SALARIYA

Published in Great Britain in MMXIII by
Book House, an imprint of
The Salariya Book Company Ltd
25 Marlborough Place, Brighton BN1 1UB

1 3 5 7 9 8 6 4 2

Please visit our website at **www.salariya.com**
for **free** electronic versions of:
You Wouldn't Want to Be an Egyptian Mummy!
You Wouldn't Want to Be a Roman Gladiator!
You Wouldn't Want to be a Polar Explorer!
You Wouldn't Want to sail on a 19th-Century Whaling Ship!

Authors:
Mark Bergin was born in Hastings in 1961.
He studied at Eastbourne College of Art and has
specialised in historical reconstructions as well as aviation
and maritime subjects since 1983. He lives in
Bexhill-on-Sea with his wife and three children.

David Antram was born in Brighton, England, in 1958.
He studied at Eastbourne College of Art and then worked in
advertising for fifteen years before becoming a full-time artist.
He has illustrated many children's non-fiction books.

Editor: Rob Walker

PB ISBN: 978-1-908759-71-9

A CIP catalogue record for this
book is available from the
British Library.

Printed and bound in China.
Printed on paper from
sustainable sources.

PAPER FROM
SUSTAINABLE
FORESTS

**WARNING: Fixatives should be
used only under adult supervision.**

@bookhousebooks   The Salariya   BookHouse100
Book Company

FIND OUR BOOKS
ON THE APP STORE:
SEARCH FOR 'SALARIYA'

Visit our **new** online shop at
shop.salariya.com
for great offers, gift ideas, all our new releases
and free postage and packaging.

DRAW
FANTASY
CHARACTERS

BOOK   HOUSE

Contents

DRAW

Drawing materials

DRAW

Try using different types of drawing papers and materials. Experiment with charcoal, wax crayons and pastels. All pens, from felt-tips to ballpoints, will make interesting marks — or try drawing with pen and ink on wet paper.

Charcoal is very soft and can be used for big, bold drawings. Ask an adult to spray your charcoal drawings with fixative to prevent smudging.

You can create special effects by scraping away parts of a drawing done with **wax crayons**.

Silhouette is a style of drawing that uses only a solid black shadow.

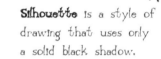

Felt-tip pens are ideal for quick sketches. If the ink is not waterproof, try drawing on wet paper and see what happens.

Felt-tips

6

Pencils

Hard **pencils** are greyer and soft pencils are blacker. Hard pencils are graded from 6H (the hardest) through 5H, 4H, 3H and 2H to H. Soft pencils are graded from B, 2B, 3B, 4B and 5B up to 6B (the softest).

Pen and ink

Pastels are even softer than charcoal, and come in a wide range of colours. Ask an adult to spray your pastel drawings with fixative to prevent smudging.

Lines drawn in **ink** cannot be erased, so keep your ink drawings sketchy and less rigid. Don't worry about mistakes as these lines can be lost in the drawing as it develops.

7

Perspective

If you look at any object from different viewpoints, you will see that the part that is closest to you looks larger, and the part furthest away from you looks smaller. Drawing in perspective is a way of creating a feeling of depth – of showing three dimensions on a flat surface.

The vanishing point (V.P.) is the place in a perspective drawing where parallel lines appear to meet. The position of the vanishing point depends on the viewer's eye level. Sometimes a low viewpoint can give your drawing added drama.

V.P.

V.P.

8

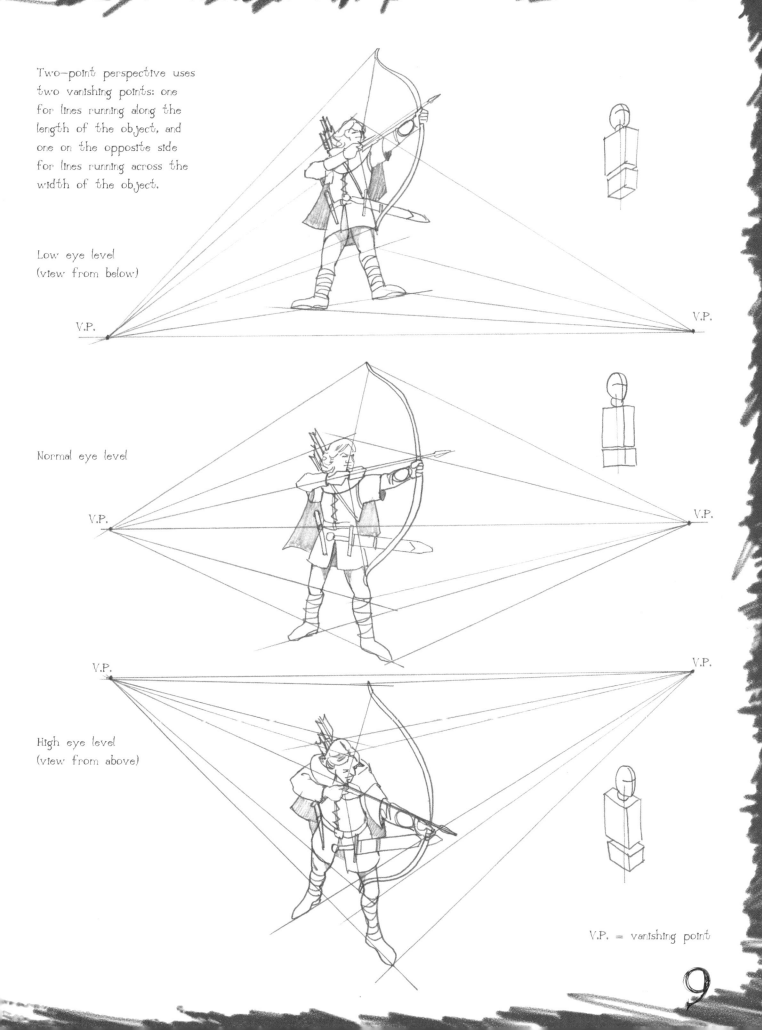

Two-point perspective uses
two vanishing points: one
for lines running along the
length of the object, and
one on the opposite side
for lines running across the
width of the object.

Low eye level
(view from below)

V.P.

V.P.

Normal eye level

V.P.

V.P.

High eye level
(view from above)

V.P.

V.P.

V.P. = vanishing point

9

Amazon warrior

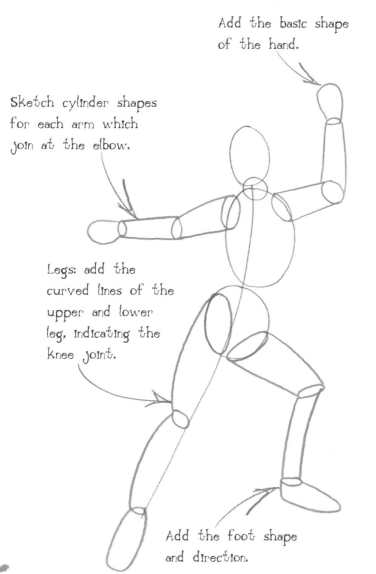

This powerful female figure is a classic action fantasy character. She must look strong and powerful but retain her femininity and beauty.

Draw in ovals for the head, neck, body and hips.

Draw a long curved line to start the position of the body.

Add the basic shape of the hand.

Sketch cylinder shapes for each arm which join at the elbow.

Legs: add the curved lines of the upper and lower leg, indicating the knee joint.

Add the foot shape and direction.

Practise sketching your own hands in different positions. This will help you draw expressive hands on your characters.

Add the sword using straight lines.

Sketch in the position of the ears, nose and mouth.

Sketch in the shape of the hair mass.

Indicate the position and shape of the breasts.

Add fingers to each hand.

Add the costume's draped cloth using simple lines.

Finish the detail on the sword. Small broken lines give the impression of shining metal.

Add tone and details to the hair.

Draw in the top of the costume.

Draw in bracelets and armbands.

Add shade to areas where the light would not reach.

Draw in the boot shapes.

Add tone to the legs.

Complete the details on the boots.

Remove any unwanted construction lines.

11

Warrior queen

This character's commanding stance oozes strength and power but still displays her femininity through her flowing cloak and costume. Her sword displays the metal-working skills of the great sword masters — the elves.

Draw ovals for the head, neck, body and hips.

Draw in a centre line.

Add cylinder shapes for each arm, showing elbow joints.

Mark the position of the eyes, nose and mouth.

Draw the position of the fingers.

Draw in the position and shape of the breasts.

Draw in the basic shape of the hands.

Draw straight lines for the legs. Indicate knee joints.

Draw in the belt, making sure it goes around the figure.

Draw in the basic shape and direction of the feet.

Sketch in the shape of the sword.

Using the same basic head shape you can create your own variety of character heads, from monster to Amazon to orc!

Add more detail to the face.

Sketch in the hood raised over the head.

Draw in the shape of the cloak with long curved lines.

Draw the fingers of the hand.

Add the shape of the bodice and sleeves.

Add shading under the hood and add the headband.

Using flowing lines, draw in the hair.

Draw in arm guards.

Add decorative details to the sword.

Use straight lines to indicate the folds in the fabric.

Shade areas where the light will not reach.

Remove any unwanted construction lines.

Finish details on the feet.

Add shadows under the hem of the dress.

13

Barbarian

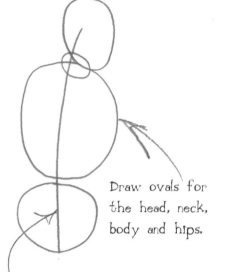

This fierce northern warrior comes from feudal warmongering tribes. He has an impressive muscular build with broad shoulders and large, powerful arms as he relies on his strength in combat. His weapons are heavy and oversized to inflict the maximum damage on his opponents.

Draw ovals for the head, neck, body and hips.

Draw in a centre line.

Draw in the shape of the hands.

Sketch in the shape of the squared shoulders and the chest.

Draw in cylinder shapes for the legs. Show knee joints.

Draw cylinder shapes for each arm showing the elbow joint.

Add the basic foot shape and direction.

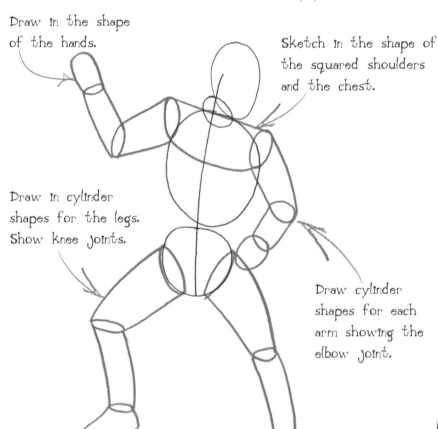

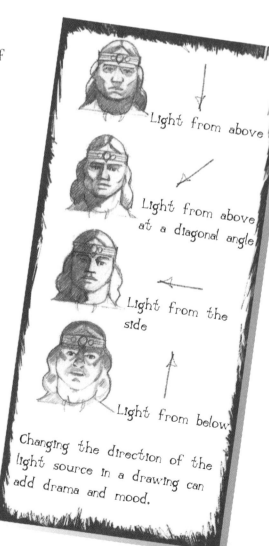

Light from above

Light from above at a diagonal angle

Light from the side

Light from below

Changing the direction of the light source in a drawing can add drama and mood.

14

Draw in the shape of the fingers.

Add the horned helmet using curved lines.

Sketch in the position of the eyes, nose and mouth.

Draw long curved lines to show the shape of the cape.

Draw the sword, scabbard and belt.

Draw in both the axe hafts.

Draw in the axe heads, embellishing them with details.

Add the details of the face, the hair and helmet.

Sketch in the tops of the boots.

Draw in decorative wrist guards.

Use curved lines to add muscles to the body.

Draw in the loincloth.

Add tone to the legs.

Finish the detail on the boots.

Remove any unwanted construction lines.

Shade in areas where light would not reach, especially the inside folds of the cloak.

15

Ogre

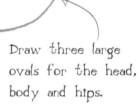

This gigantic and formidable bloated monster has only one thing on his mind — gluttony. His victims' heads are slung gruesomely around his belt to become the ingredients of his next meal! His weapon is a massive club — a great meat tenderiser!

Draw a centre line for the figure.

Draw three large ovals for the head, body and hips.

Draw in the arms. Keep them in proportion to the body.

Sketch in the shape of the hands.

Sketch in the legs, making them quite thick and short. Show the knee joints.

Draw in the shape and direction of both large feet.

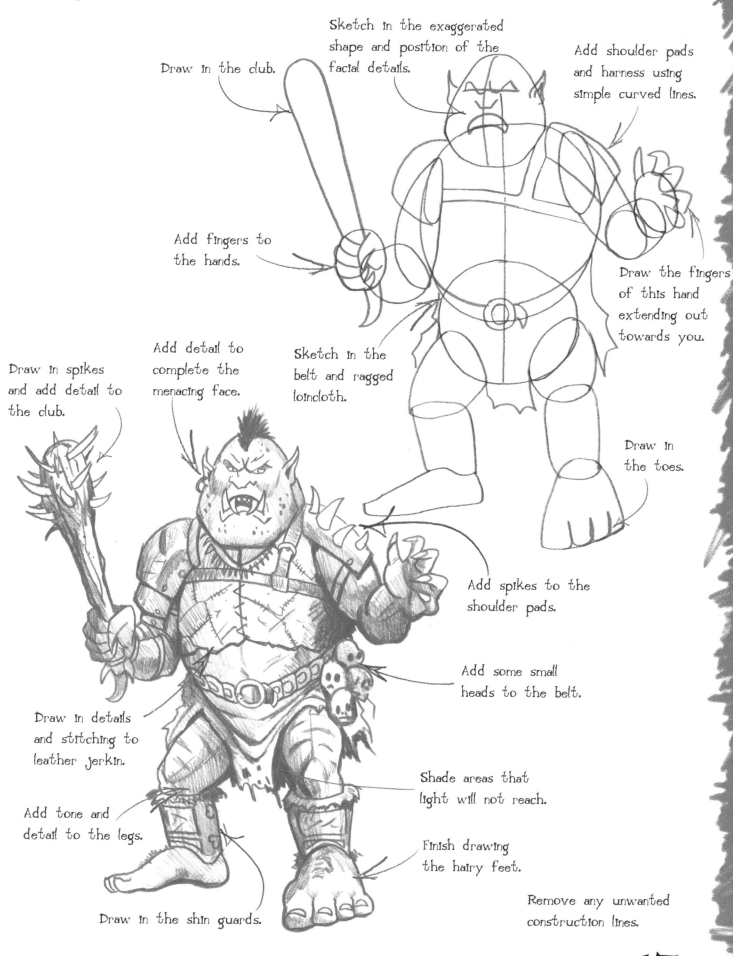

Draw in the club.

Sketch in the exaggerated shape and position of the facial details.

Add shoulder pads and harness using simple curved lines.

Add fingers to the hands.

Draw the fingers of this hand extending out towards you.

Draw in spikes and add detail to the club.

Add detail to complete the menacing face.

Sketch in the belt and ragged loincloth.

Add spikes to the shoulder pads.

Draw in the toes.

Add some small heads to the belt.

Draw in details and stitching to leather jerkin.

Shade areas that light will not reach.

Add tone and detail to the legs.

Finish drawing the hairy feet.

Draw in the shin guards.

Remove any unwanted construction lines.

17

Undead warrior

This once proud warrior has turned, in death, into a hideous and terrifying evil demon. His head is reduced to a skull and flesh hangs from his body. He is summoned up to collect the souls of dead warriors on the battlefield.

Draw ovals for the head, neck, body and hips.

Draw in a centre line.

Sketch in the shape and position of the arms with cylinder shapes. Show elbow joints.

Add basic shapes for the hands.

Sketch in the legs, showing the knee joints.

Draw in the feet pointing down.

Draw lots of small figures to find the best action pose. Try out poses yourself in front of a mirror to see what looks good.

Draw in the sword using long curved lines for the blade.

Sketch in the head details: the facial structure and the helmet.

Draw in the scabbard, sword and belt.

Draw circles for the shield.

Draw a small axe tucked in the belt.

Sketch the start of the bandages on the legs.

Add detail to the face and helmet.

Add detail to the armour.

Make the sword look shiny by drawing straight lines across the length of the blade.

Add the details of the body.

Add gruesome detail to the legs: bones showing through the flesh.

Add detail and tone to the shield.

Shade areas that light will not reach.

Remove any unwanted construction lines.

Finish drawing the bandages round the legs.

19

DRAW Winged avenger

This dynamic female angel hunts out evil 'on the wing'. Her wings are her most powerful limbs. She uses magic weapons and a shield to protect and defend herself against the evil forces that vie against her.

Draw ovals for the head, neck, body and hips.

Sketch a centre line that continues through the extended leg.

Draw cylinder shapes for the arms, showing the elbow joints.

Sketch in the basic shape of the hands.

Sketch the positions of the facial features.

Indicate the position and shape of the breasts.

Sketch in the position of the raised leg and foot.

Add curved lines to the torso, dividing up each section of clothing and body.

Add the trailing leg and foot using the centre line as a guide.

Sketch in the position of the wings using long curved lines.

Add more facial details.

Draw in the shape of the shield.

Draw the weapon clasped in her hand.

Sketch in the shape of the trailing leg.

Draw in wing features using carefully curved lines.

Draw in the flowing hair.

Shade areas that light will not reach.

Add detail and tone to the shield.

Complete all details on the torso and costume.

Add flowing drapery.

Add all finishing details to the boots.

Remove any unwanted construction lines.

DRAW
War wizard

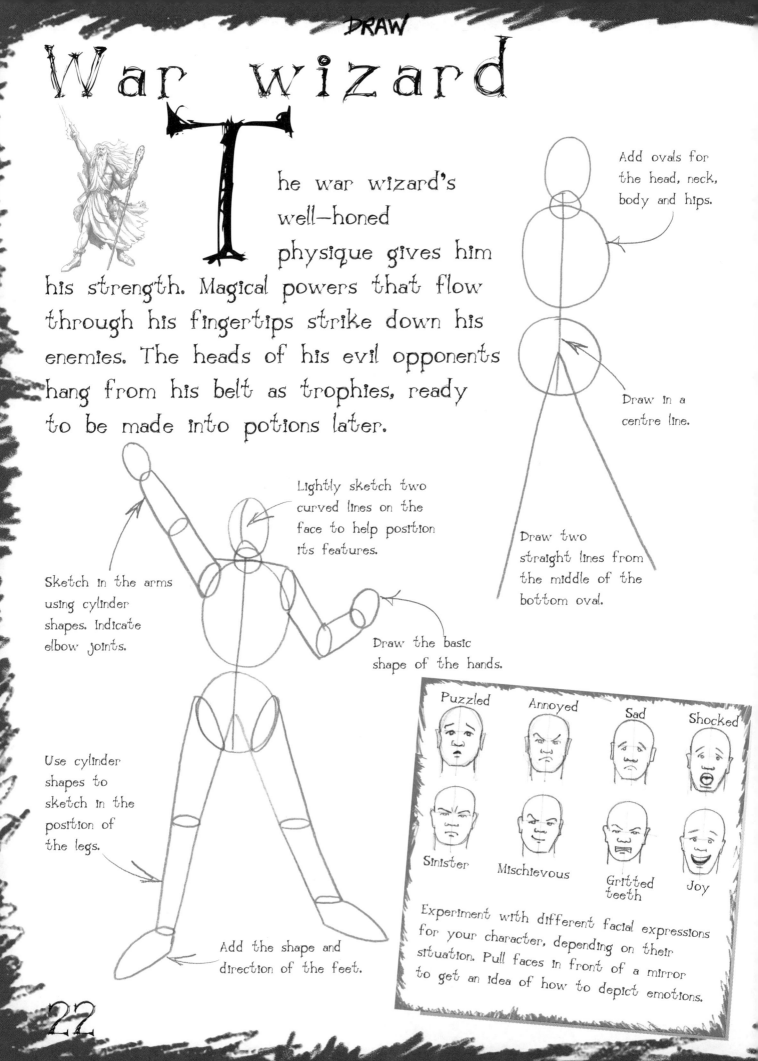

The war wizard's well—honed physique gives him his strength. Magical powers that flow through his fingertips strike down his enemies. The heads of his evil opponents hang from his belt as trophies, ready to be made into potions later.

Add ovals for the head, neck, body and hips.

Draw in a centre line.

Draw two straight lines from the middle of the bottom oval.

Lightly sketch two curved lines on the face to help position its features.

Sketch in the arms using cylinder shapes. Indicate elbow joints.

Draw the basic shape of the hands.

Use cylinder shapes to sketch in the position of the legs.

Add the shape and direction of the feet.

Puzzled   Annoyed   Sad   Shocked

Sinister   Mischievous   Gritted teeth   Joy

Experiment with different facial expressions for your character, depending on their situation. Pull faces in front of a mirror to get an idea of how to depict emotions.

Draw in the hand details with a finger pointed upwards.

Add in the basic shape of the hair mass and the beard.

Sketch in the positions of the eyes, nose and mouth.

Draw jagged lines around the hand to show his magical powers.

Sketch in the sword and belt.

Draw in the wizard's staff.

Draw in all the facial details.

Use curved lines to add detail to the wizard's hair.

Draw in remaining details of the torso.

Draw in the wizard's robe using long curved lines.

Add head 'trophies' to his belt.

Add detail to the staff and sword.

Complete the robe using tone to show folds. Add jagged lines to show the tattered edges.

Draw in the wizard's boots

Add shading to areas that light does not reach, particularly to the inside of the robe.

Remove any unwanted construction lines.

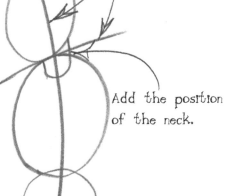

Goblin

This evil and devious creature is a fierce fighter. He will be found in dark mountain areas where great goblin armies scheme and plan their battles against the dwarf lords. They are not the strongest opponents but they overwhelm their enemies by their great numbers.

Draw in a centre line with another crossing it.

Add the position of the neck.

Draw three ovals for the head, body and hips.

Sketch in the position of the facial features.

Add pointed ears.

Draw a long straight line for the spear shaft.

Sketch three ovals for shoulders and arms.

Draw curved lines for the shape of the legs.

Draw two ovals for the shape of the hand.

Sketch in circles for the knees and ankles.

Draw in the shape and direction of the feet.

24

Start to add the facial features.

Draw in the hair strip.

Add another long straight line to the spear shaft.

Draw in the bow and quiver which are slung behind him.

Draw in the armour on the torso.

Add the loincloth.

Draw in the clawed fingers.

Add in the goblin's knee and shin guards.

Complete the scary facial features.

Draw in the sharp spearhead using straight lines.

Add arrows to the quiver.

Draw in leggings.

Add clawed toenails.

Finish drawing the details of the armour and belt.

Finish details on the leg armour.

Add ragged edges to the loincloth.

Add shade to areas where the light would not reach.

Remove any unwanted construction lines.

DRAW
Goblin vs. warrior

Draw this action fighting scene: the crouching goblin is ready to strike at the upright stance of the brave, defending warrior who towers over him. Always remember to sketch in your initial drawing lightly so that you can add in more detail later.

Draw a centre line for each figure.

Sketch in ovals for the head, neck, body and hips of each figure.

Draw in the basic shape of the hands.

Sketch in a straight line for the position of the shoulders.

Draw the arms of each figure using simple cylinder shapes.

Draw in the shape and direction of each foot.

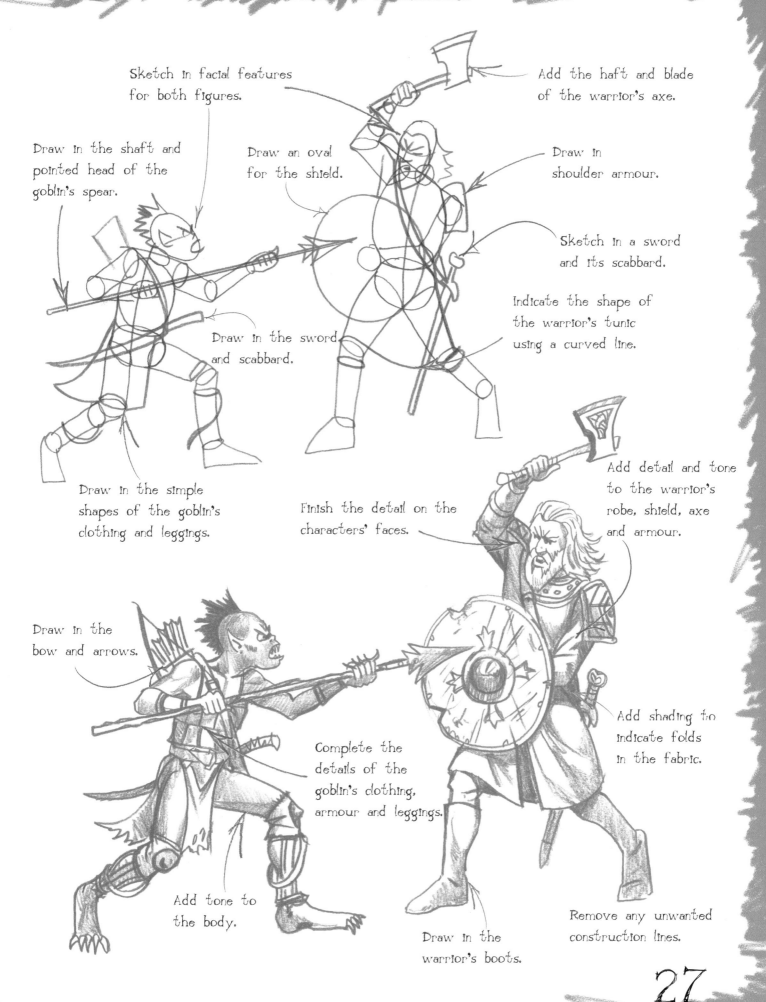

Sketch in facial features for both figures.

Draw in the shaft and pointed head of the goblin's spear.

Draw an oval for the shield.

Add the haft and blade of the warrior's axe.

Draw in shoulder armour.

Draw in the sword and scabbard.

Sketch in a sword and its scabbard.

Indicate the shape of the warrior's tunic using a curved line.

Draw in the simple shapes of the goblin's clothing and leggings.

Finish the detail on the characters' faces.

Add detail and tone to the warrior's robe, shield, axe and armour.

Draw in the bow and arrows.

Complete the details of the goblin's clothing, armour and leggings.

Add shading to indicate folds in the fabric.

Add tone to the body.

Draw in the warrior's boots.

Remove any unwanted construction lines.

27

Centaur

A centaur is half horse, half man. Centaurs were said to have come from the mountains of Thessaly in Greece, and were wild, lawless and savage. The Greek hero Heracles killed centaurs with poison—tipped arrows.

Draw in a rectangle for the centaur's chest.

Man body

Draw two circles to form the body.

Draw in centre line

Horse body

Draw in lines for the back and the belly.

Draw the ground the centaur stands on.

Draw a line for the spear.

Head

Spear

Draw a small circle for a head and two lines to form a neck.

Arm

Add lines for the legs and arms, with circles for the joints, hands and hooves.

Front legs

Back legs

28

Indicate the positions of the eyes, nose and mouth.

Add hair to the centaur's head.

Draw in the muscles of the upper body.

Draw in the muscles of the lower body, and curved lines to show the position of the tail.

Add detail to the centaur's hands.

Draw in the detail of the spear.

Finish drawing in the eyes, nose and mouth.

Shade in the muscles.

Pencil lines should follow the direction of the tail.

Take a look at real horses' legs.

Composition

Use squares or rectangles to frame your composition. This can make all the difference.

29

Dragon

Dragons are thought to have magical and spiritual powers, and are common to many cultures of the world. These cunning creatures typically have scaly bodies, wings and fiery breath. The Chinese consider them symbols of good luck.

Draw a circle to form the head, and a larger oval for the main body.

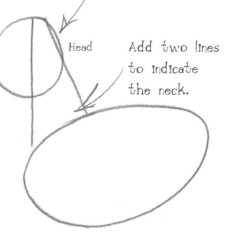

Head

Add two lines to indicate the neck.

Main body

Sketch in shapes for the top of the head and the lower jaw.

Draw in lines for the wing base and circles for the joints.

Add a long curved line to show the position of the tail.

Head

Draw triangular shapes to indicate the positions of the feet.

Add lines for front and rear legs, with circles for the joints.

The use of light and dark to create bold images is called chiaroscuro. Try this on the dragon to get more impact.

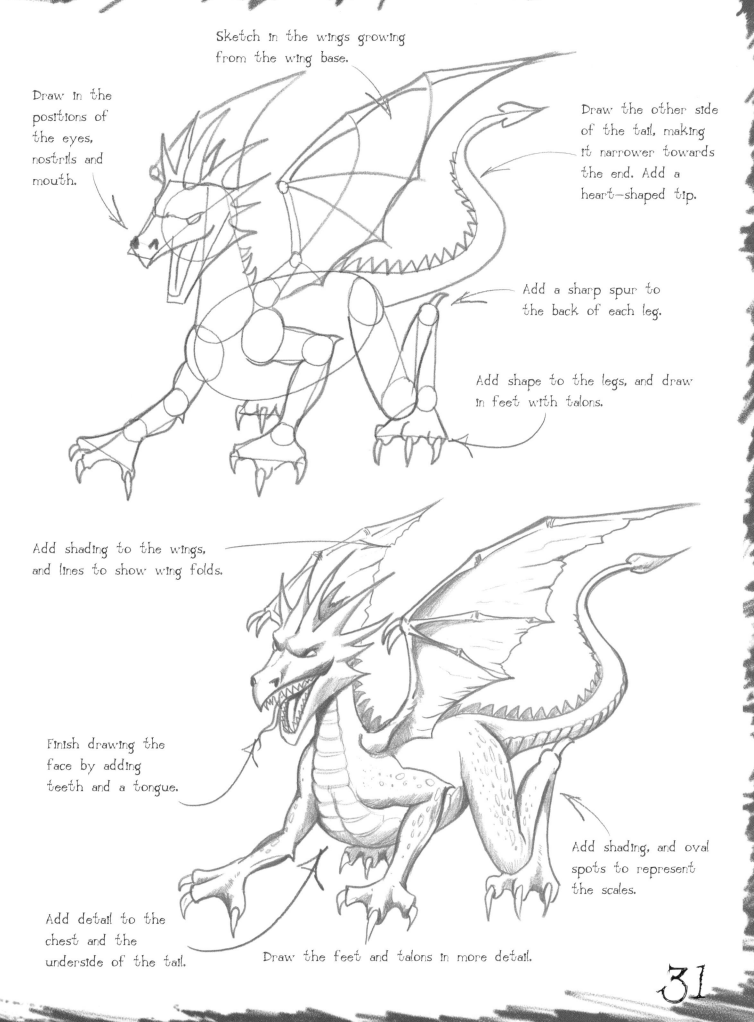

Sketch in the wings growing from the wing base.

Draw in the positions of the eyes, nostrils and mouth.

Draw the other side of the tail, making it narrower towards the end. Add a heart-shaped tip.

Add a sharp spur to the back of each leg.

Add shape to the legs, and draw in feet with talons.

Add shading to the wings, and lines to show wing folds.

Finish drawing the face by adding teeth and a tongue.

Add detail to the chest and the underside of the tail.

Draw the feet and talons in more detail.

Add shading, and oval spots to represent the scales.

31

Gryphon

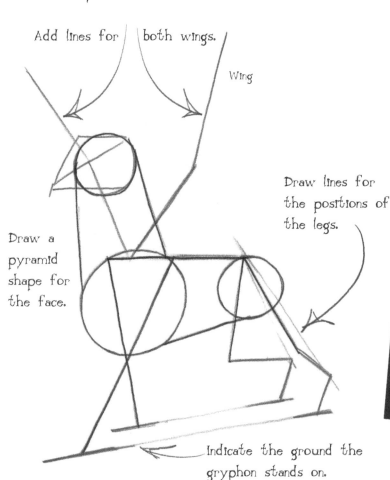

The gryphon (griffin) or lion—eagle was considered to be the king of the air, and was a powerful and majestic creature. In Persian culture, gryphons are shown drawing the sun across the sky.

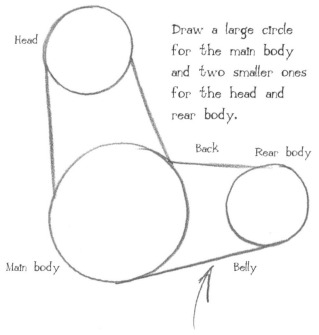

Head

Back

Rear body

Main body

Belly

Draw a large circle for the main body and two smaller ones for the head and rear body.

Draw in lines for the neck and for the back and belly.

Add lines for both wings.

Wing

Draw a pyramid shape for the face.

Draw lines for the positions of the legs.

Indicate the ground the gryphon stands on.

Look at the space around the figure (negative space) to help check the proportions and shape of your drawing.

Wing construction

First draw two straight lines.

Add two oval shapes.

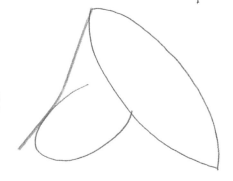

Carefully sketch in the beak, then add ears and eyes.

Draw in a shield-like shape at the base of the body.

Add a curved, lion-like tail.

Tail

Add detail of back feet and legs.

Sketch in the front feet.

Add muscles to the wing.

Indicate the groups of feathers.

Carefully draw in rows of feathers.

Add shading under the front edge of the wing.

Finish drawing the detail of the gryphon's head.

Use short downward strokes to draw the chest feathers.

Add wing features (see left).

Add shading.

Add hair to the tip of the tail.

Draw the sharp eagle's talons.

Hydra

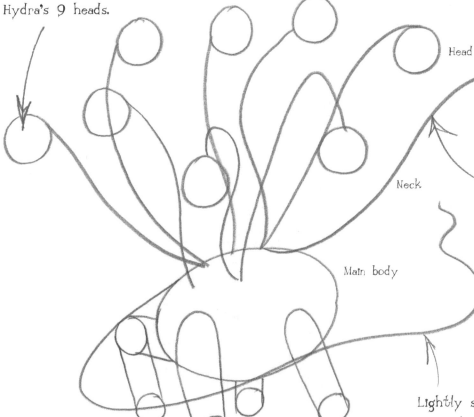

The Hydra in Greek mythology was said to guard the entrance to the underworld beneath the waters of Lake Lerna. Heracles killed this hideous creature as one of his twelve labours.

Add two lines to join this leg to the body.

Draw a large oval for the main body.

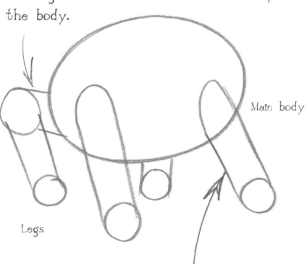

Main body

Legs

Draw four tube shapes for the legs.

Draw a circle for each of the Hydra's 9 heads.

Head

Neck

Main body

Draw long, curvy neck lines from the back of each head to the body.

Lightly sketch in a long, wavy line for the tail.

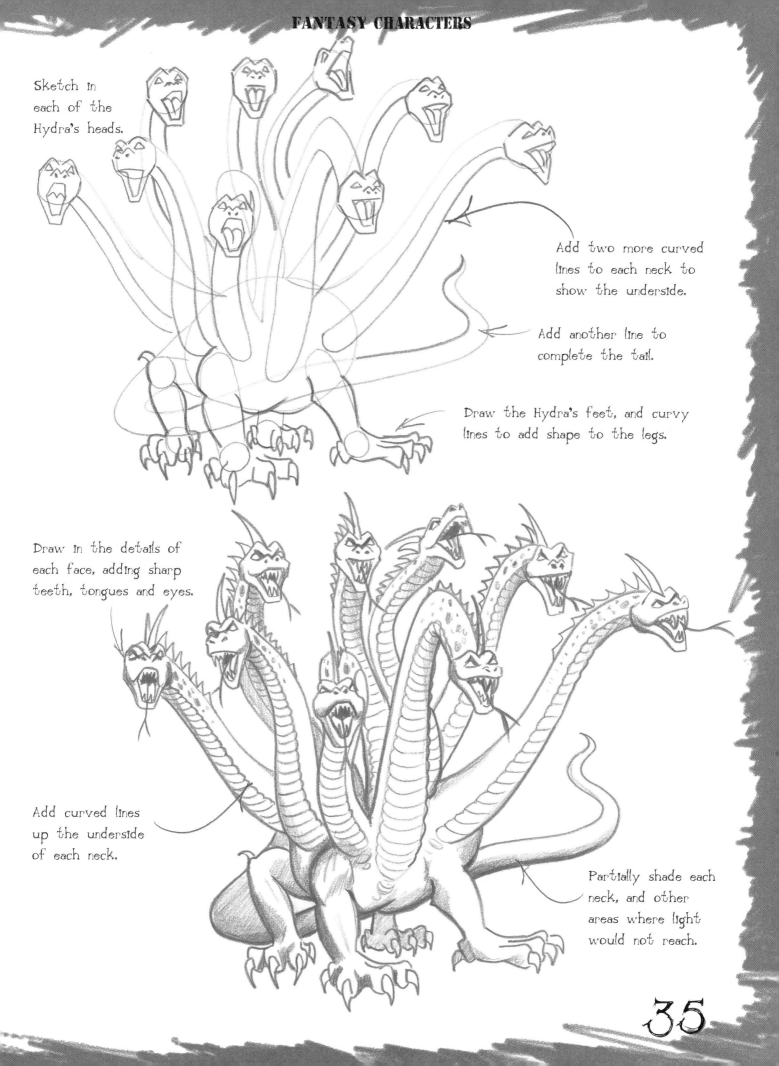

Sketch in each of the Hydra's heads.

Add two more curved lines to each neck to show the underside.

Add another line to complete the tail.

Draw the Hydra's feet, and curvy lines to add shape to the legs.

Draw in the details of each face, adding sharp teeth, tongues and eyes.

Add curved lines up the underside of each neck.

Partially shade each neck, and other areas where light would not reach.

35

Minotaur

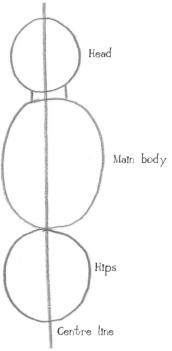

The Minotaur was half man, half bull. This creature of Greek myth was said to dwell in the labyrinth constructed by King Minos at Knossos. Theseus eventually killed the beast, then found his way out safely by following the trail of string he had left to guide him.

Draw a vertical line through the centre.

Sketch in two circles and an oval to form the head, main body and hips.

Head

Main body

Hips

Centre line

Centre line

Head

Arms

Draw a line to indicate the top of the shoulders.

Sketch two ovals, one smaller and overlapping the other, to show the right arm bent at the elbow. Add a circle for the hand.

Draw a straight line passing through the hand shapes for the axe haft.

Hips

Sketch a long oval shape with a roundish oval below it to show the foreshortening of the left arm. Add a smaller overlapping circle for the hand.

Draw a large oval for each thigh. Add two lines to join these to smaller ovals which form the lower legs. Add circles at the end of each leg for ankles, and sketch in the hooves with two semicircles.

Thigh

Lower leg

Ankle

Hoof

36

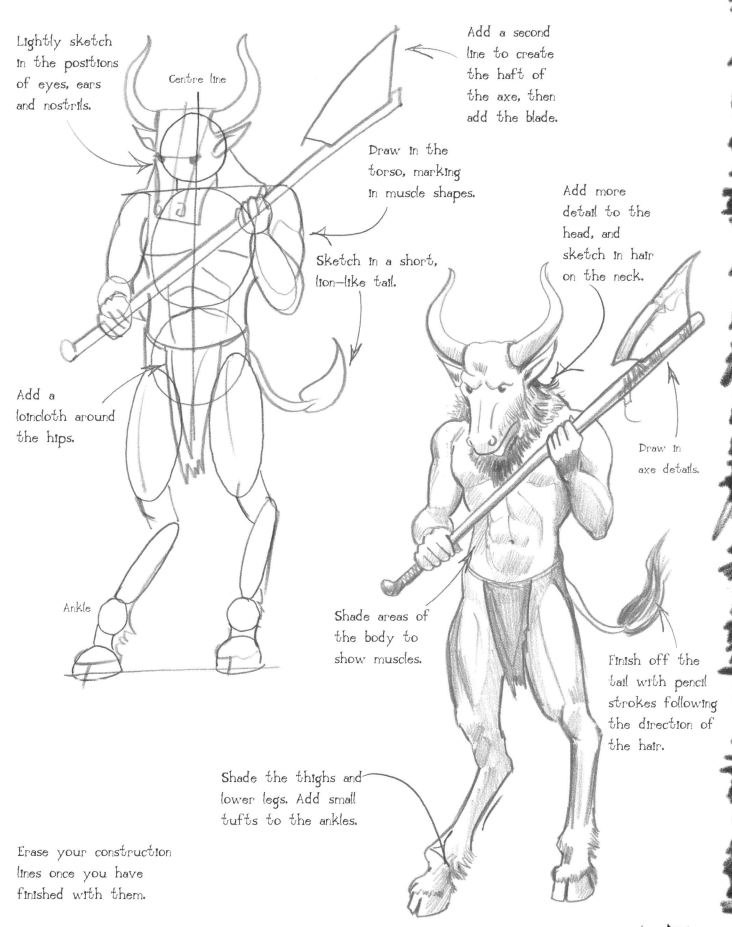

Lightly sketch in the positions of eyes, ears and nostrils.

Centre line

Add a second line to create the haft of the axe, then add the blade.

Draw in the torso, marking in muscle shapes.

Add more detail to the head, and sketch in hair on the neck.

Sketch in a short, lion-like tail.

Add a loincloth around the hips.

Draw in axe details.

Ankle

Shade areas of the body to show muscles.

Finish off the tail with pencil strokes following the direction of the hair.

Shade the thighs and lower legs. Add small tufts to the ankles.

Erase your construction lines once you have finished with them.

37

Pegasus

Pegasus, the Greek winged horse, was said to have been born from the blood spilt by Medusa's murder. Pegasus aided the Greek hero Bellerophon against the Chimera and the Amazons. He also brought thunderbolts to Zeus, the king of the gods.

Draw a triangle shape for the neck and a circle for the head.

Head

Back

Rear

Belly

Draw two circles, one slightly larger than the other, for the body. Add lines for the back and belly.

Draw three lines from the head and another line across to form the muzzle.

Draw a crooked line to indicate the front wing base.

Sketch in a V-shaped line to show the base of the neck.

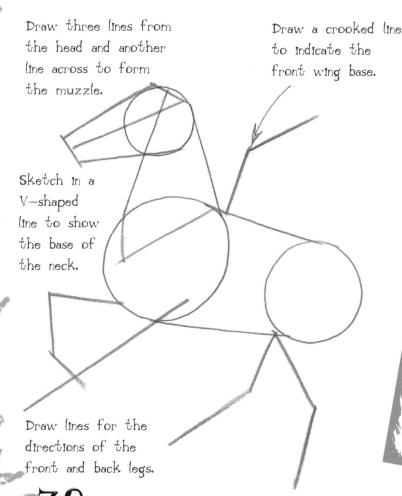

Draw lines for the directions of the front and back legs.

To keep the object you are drawing in proportion, choose a unit of measurement that you can relate back to. Here the width of Pegasus has been divided into three. You can also mark key points in the drawing to take measurements from.

Wings

Draw a bent line for the front of the wing.

Draw a simple curved shape for the main part.

Add the inner part of the wing.

Indicate the rows of feathers.

Neatly draw in the overlapping feathers.

Sketch in the horse's eyes, mouth, nostrils and ears. Add a mane.

Draw in wing shapes.

Indicate the flowing tail.

Draw in more lines to give the legs shape. Add circles for joints.

Add more detail to the horse's head.

Draw small wing feathers first, then longer feathers.

Shade in the muscle shape.

Add more detail to the tail.

Shade in the underside of Pegasus to create a three-dimensional effect.

Phoenix

The phoenix is a mythical bird said to live for up to 1,461 years. It has red and gold plumage. Each time it nears the end of its life, the phoenix builds a nest of cinnamon twigs that ignites. Both the bird and its nest are turned into ashes, from which a new phoenix arises.

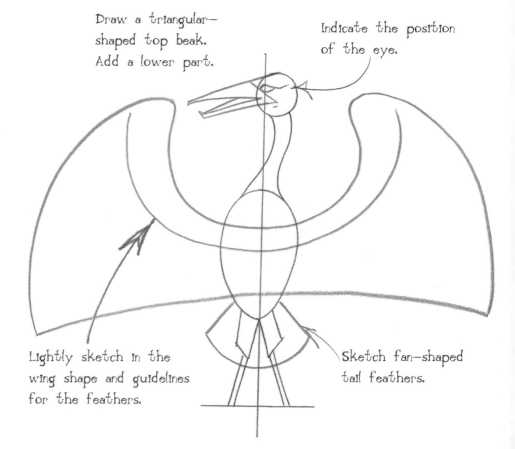

Draw a vertical line to mark the centre of the phoenix.

Sketch a small circle for the head.

Draw a large oval for the body.

Draw two curved lines almost parallel for the neck.

Draw thin legs splayed outwards. The tops of the legs look like short trousers.

Draw a triangular-shaped top beak. Add a lower part.

Indicate the position of the eye.

Lightly sketch in the wing shape and guidelines for the feathers.

Sketch fan-shaped tail feathers.

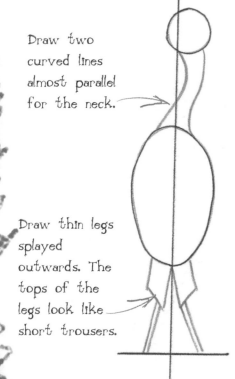

Add a plume of feathers to the back of the head.

Draw in the large lower feathers.

Carefully sketch in the front of the wings.

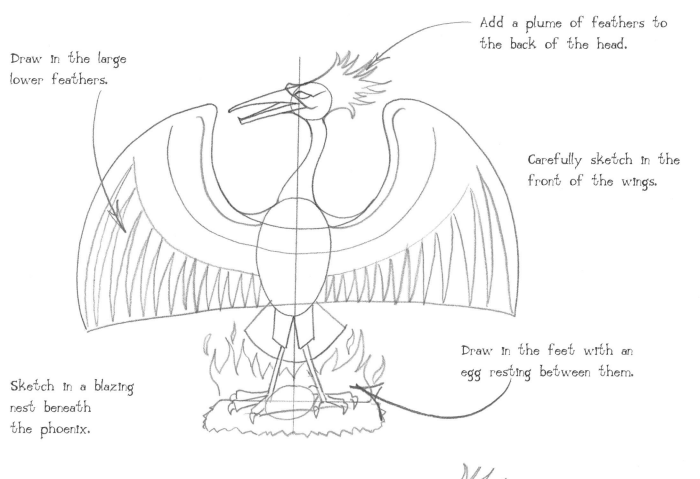

Sketch in a blazing nest beneath the phoenix.

Draw in the feet with an egg resting between them.

Draw two more rows of feathers on the wings.

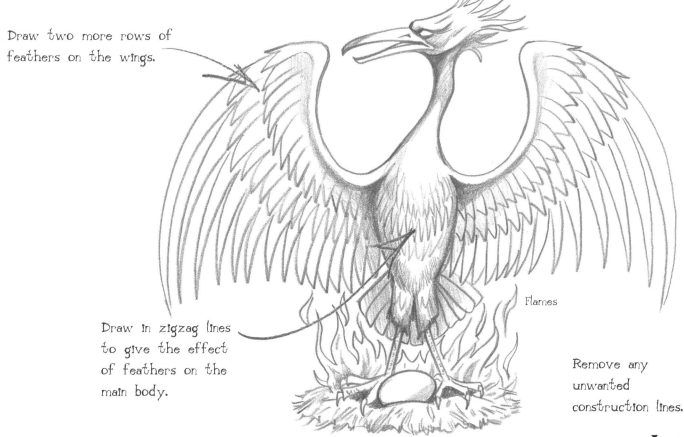

Flames

Draw in zigzag lines to give the effect of feathers on the main body.

Remove any unwanted construction lines.

41

Troll

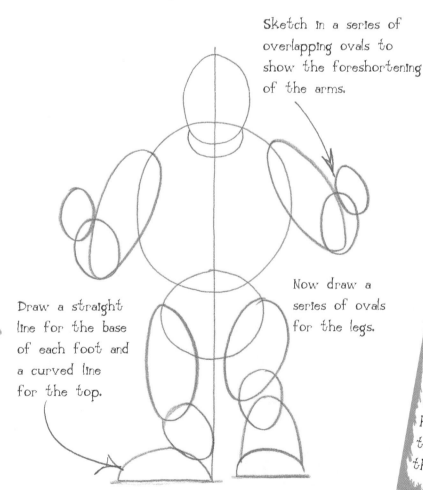

The large mountain troll features in many folk tales. They are said to be foul-smelling creatures that are dim-witted but powerful. Trolls are aggressive towards humans and carry a crude, primitive club as a weapon.

First draw a centre line.

Head

Body

Hips

Draw a large circle for the body. Draw two smaller circles overlapping at top and bottom for the head and hips.

Sketch in a series of overlapping ovals to show the foreshortening of the arms.

Now draw a series of ovals for the legs.

Draw a straight line for the base of each foot and a curved line for the top.

To draw the face, first draw a line down the centre of the head, then two horizontal lines to help you construct the face. The top horizontal line shows the position of the eyes, the top of the nose and where the ears join the head. The bottom horizontal line shows the base of the nose and the bottom of the ears.

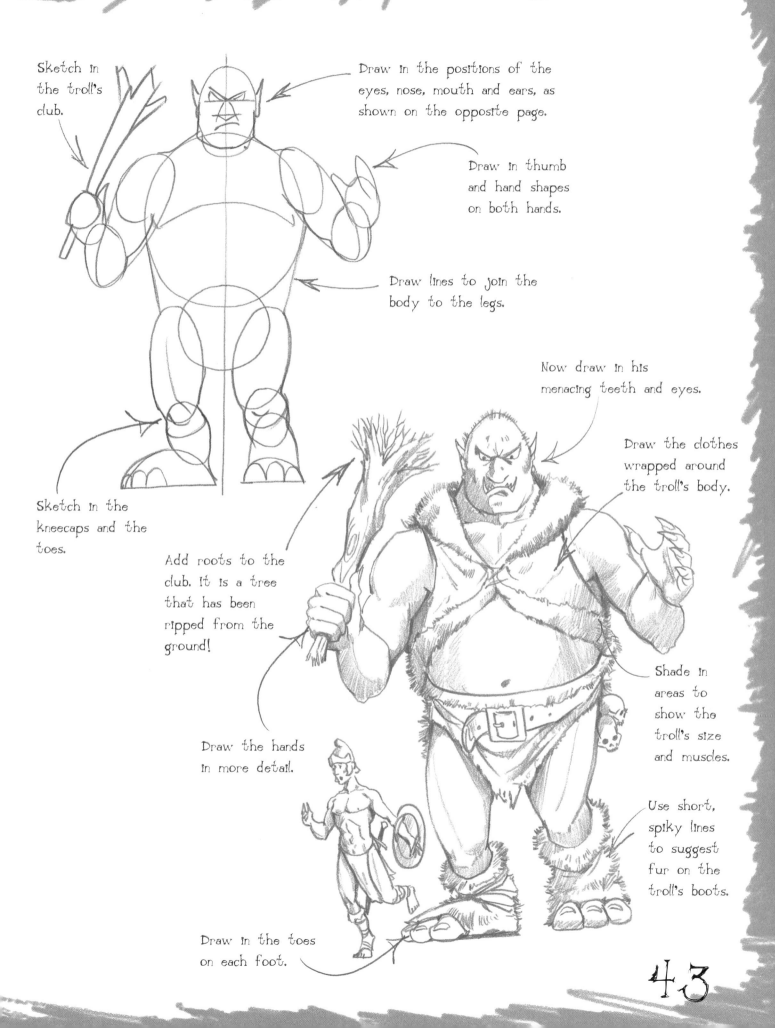

Sketch in the troll's club.

Draw in the positions of the eyes, nose, mouth and ears, as shown on the opposite page.

Draw in thumb and hand shapes on both hands.

Draw lines to join the body to the legs.

Now draw in his menacing teeth and eyes.

Draw the clothes wrapped around the troll's body.

Sketch in the kneecaps and the toes.

Add roots to the club. It is a tree that has been ripped from the ground!

Shade in areas to show the troll's size and muscles.

Use short, spiky lines to suggest fur on the troll's boots.

Draw the hands in more detail.

Draw in the toes on each foot.

43

Unicorn

The unicorn is a fabulous horse with a twisted horn on its head. It is said to be fierce yet good, a selfless, solitary but always beautiful creature. The ancient Greeks thought that unicorns lived in India.

Above the body, draw a circle for the head, and two lines to form the neck.

Head

Back

Rear

Front

Belly

First draw two circles, one slightly larger than the other. Draw in lines for the back and the belly.

Sketch in the muzzle by drawing a smaller circle and then joining it to the head with two lines.

Add ears.

Curved lines around the body and the base of the neck make your drawing look more three-dimensional.

Hold your picture up to a mirror to look at its reflection. This will help you see any mistakes in your drawing.

Draw in the legs, using circles to show the positions of the joints.

Curve the belly line upwards.

The hooves are semicircles.

Make your construction lines curved to show the unicorn's muscle structure.

Sketch in the eyes, nostrils and horn. Add the unicorn's mane.

Draw more detail on the unicorn's horn.

Sketch in the shape of the tail.

The mane is drawn using random jagged shapes flowing backwards.

Add more detail to the head.

Draw in the tail hair with curved lines flowing backwards.

Add detail and shading to the hooves. Leave some areas white as highlights.

Shade in areas where light does not reach to give a three-dimensional look.

45

DRAW Super-strong man

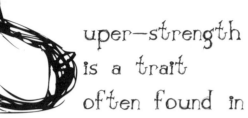

Super-strength is a trait often found in super heroes. This character fights evil using his strength to overcome all odds. Here he can be seen lifting a huge boulder over his head.

Draw in a straight line for the character's spine.

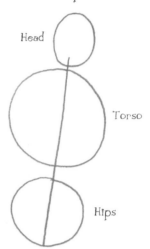

Head

Torso

Hips

Add three circles for the head, torso and hips. Make the torso shape larger.

Add a small circle for each shoulder.

Add powerful thighs coming out from the hip circle.

Draw cylindrical shapes for the position of each arm.

Draw in the shape of the lower legs, overlapping them with the thighs where the knee joints would be.

Sketch in the basic shape and direction of the feet.

Draw a teardrop shape for each hand, remembering to think about how the hands would grasp the boulder.

Mark the position of the facial features.

Draw in the basic shape of the figure's torso.

Draw in a large, rugged boulder.

Give your drawing added action by adding small fragments of rock falling off the boulder.

Complete the details of the hero's face and torso. Make sure he has a well-defined muscle structure under his costume.

Draw a large shadow under the hero, as the huge boulder casts a shadow too.

47

Mutant figure
DRAW

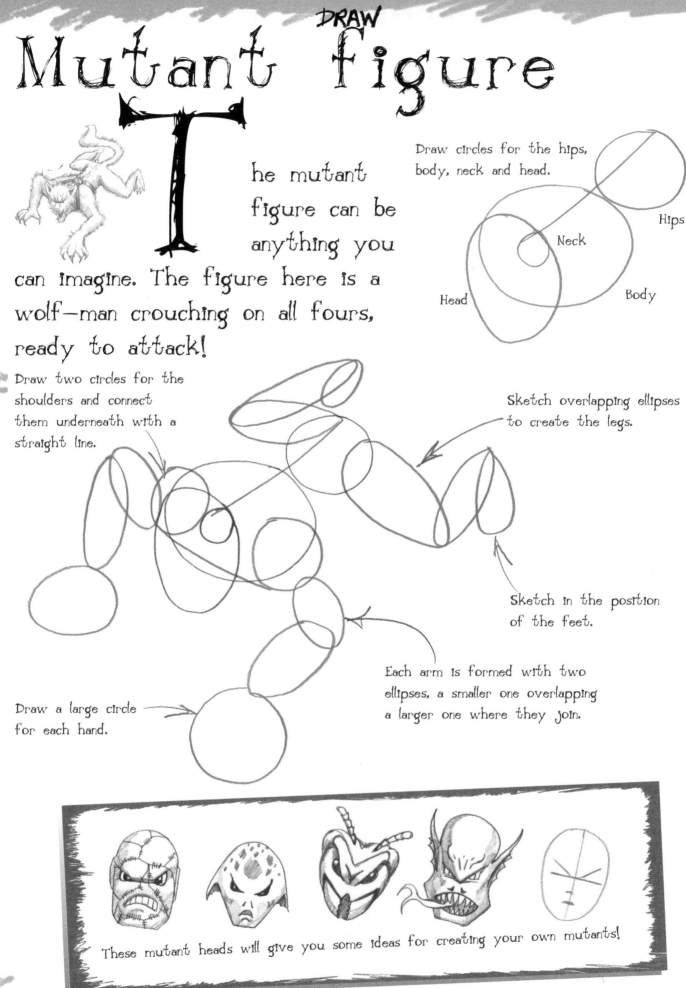

The mutant figure can be anything you can imagine. The figure here is a wolf—man crouching on all fours, ready to attack!

Draw circles for the hips, body, neck and head.

Hips

Neck

Head

Body

Draw two circles for the shoulders and connect them underneath with a straight line.

Sketch overlapping ellipses to create the legs.

Sketch in the position of the feet.

Draw a large circle for each hand.

Each arm is formed with two ellipses, a smaller one overlapping a larger one where they join.

These mutant heads will give you some ideas for creating your own mutants!

48

Sketch in small jagged lines around the outlines of the wolf-man to indicate fur.

Draw in two curved lines for the tail.

Sketch in the basic facial features.

Add claw shapes to the back feet.

Add V-shaped ears to the head.

Draw in the wolf-man's sharp, pointed claws.

Complete the feet details.

Draw small overlapping lines to create the look of fur.

Draw in the wolf-man's leather harness.

Finish all the facial details.

49

Cyborg

A cyborg is a combination of man and machine! With its mechanical additions the cyborg is far faster and stronger than a normal human being.

Head

Torso

Hips

Draw in simple shapes for the head, torso and hips with a curved line for the spine. Add a line for the direction of the shoulders.

Sketch in construction lines to give shape and direction to the head.

Draw an oval for the hand.

Extend the direction of the shoulder line forward. Now draw in a long tube, using perspective, for the outstretched cybernetic arm.

Draw rounded overlapping shapes for the legs.

Add the shape and direction of each foot.

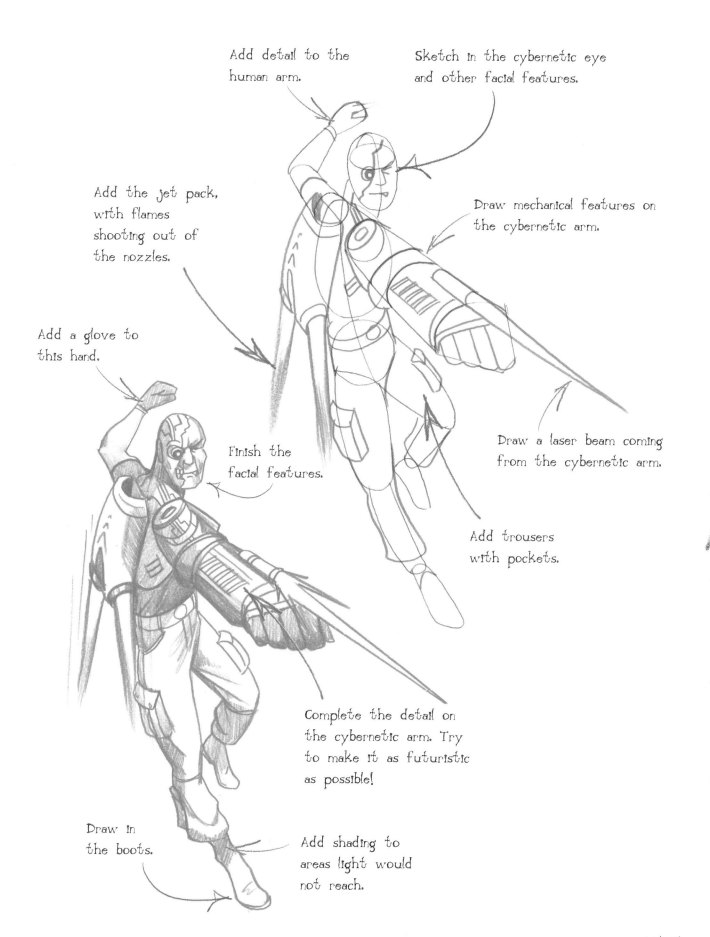

Add detail to the human arm.

Sketch in the cybernetic eye and other facial features.

Add the jet pack, with flames shooting out of the nozzles.

Draw mechanical features on the cybernetic arm.

Add a glove to this hand.

Finish the facial features.

Draw a laser beam coming from the cybernetic arm.

Add trousers with pockets.

Complete the detail on the cybernetic arm. Try to make it as futuristic as possible!

Draw in the boots.

Add shading to areas light would not reach.

Adventurous Fairies

Fairies are shy and secretive, rarely revealing themselves to humans. However, if you are lucky, one of the more adventurous ones may let you hold her on your hand.

Draw an oval shape for the fairy's head.

Head

Mark the centre of the head with two lines.

Body

Draw ovals for the body and hips.

Add lines for the arms and legs with dots for the joints. Draw in lines for the spine, shoulders and hips.

Hips

Draw triangular shapes for the feet.

Roughly sketch the shape of your hand.

Sketch in the position of the facial features.

Join the body and the hips, to get the shape of the body.

Draw in the arms and legs using simple tube shapes.

Draw in the shape of the thumb and the wrist.

Draw in the fingers using simple tube shapes.

Add the finger joints.

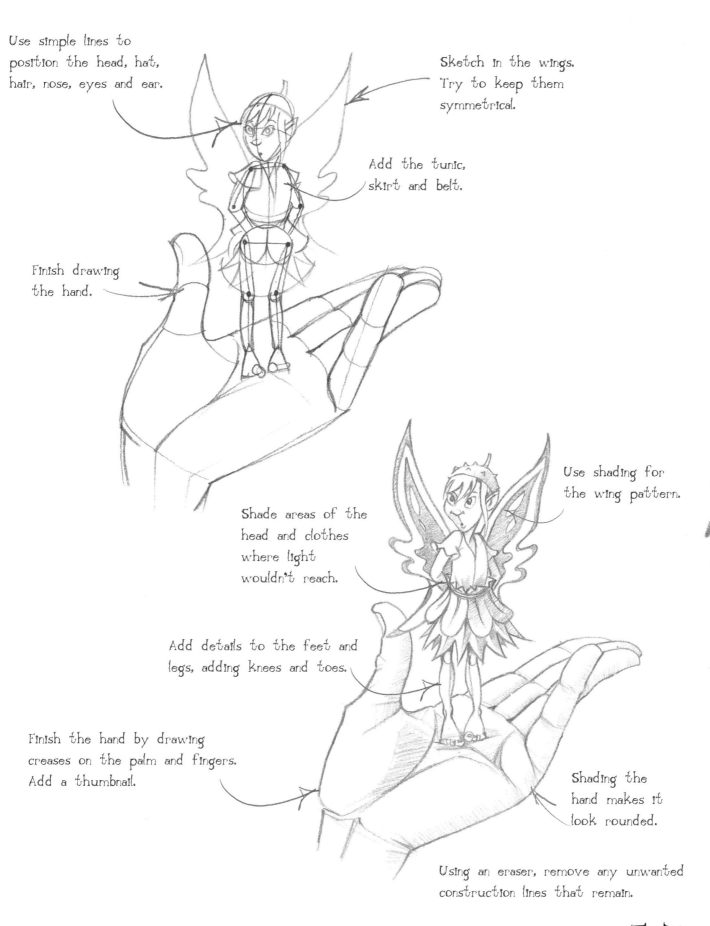

Use simple lines to position the head, hat, hair, nose, eyes and ear.

Sketch in the wings. Try to keep them symmetrical.

Add the tunic, skirt and belt.

Finish drawing the hand.

Use shading for the wing pattern.

Shade areas of the head and clothes where light wouldn't reach.

Add details to the feet and legs, adding knees and toes.

Finish the hand by drawing creases on the palm and fingers. Add a thumbnail.

Shading the hand makes it look rounded.

Using an eraser, remove any unwanted construction lines that remain.

53

Naughty Fairies

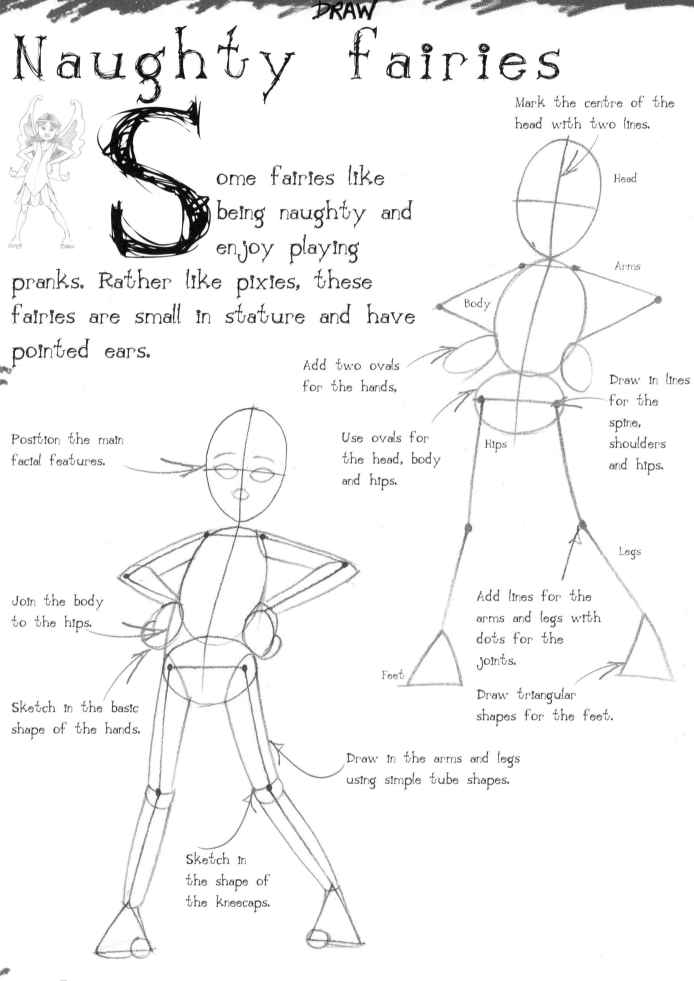

Some fairies like being naughty and enjoy playing pranks. Rather like pixies, these fairies are small in stature and have pointed ears.

Mark the centre of the head with two lines.

Head

Arms

Body

Draw in lines for the spine, shoulders and hips.

Add two ovals for the hands,

Use ovals for the head, body and hips.

Hips

Position the main facial features.

Join the body to the hips.

Legs

Add lines for the arms and legs with dots for the joints.

Feet

Draw triangular shapes for the feet.

Sketch in the basic shape of the hands.

Draw in the arms and legs using simple tube shapes.

Sketch in the shape of the kneecaps.

54

Sketch in the wings so they follow the line of the figure.

Add more detail to the face and sketch in the neck and pointed ears.

Draw in the hair and the outline of the clothes.

Add more detail to the hair and finish the face.

Curl the wings at their base for a three-dimensional effect.

Shading the wing pattern makes the fairy shape stand out.

Finish drawing the knees and ankles. and add the toes.

Look at the shapes left between the lines of your drawing known as negative space; this can help you spot mistakes.

Draw veins on the petals that form the skirt.

Finish drawing the toes. Add toenails.

Shade areas like this where light wouldn't reach.

Remove any unwanted construction lines.

Punk <small>DRAW</small> fairies

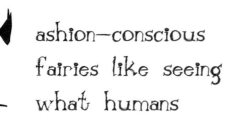

Fashion—conscious fairies like seeing what humans wear and often adapt a particular style to suit themselves. Many young fairies have been spotted in punk outfits, with their colourfully dyed, spiky hair.

Mark the centre of the head with two lines.

Draw in lines for the spine, shoulders and hips.

Draw oval shapes for the head, body and hips.

Add lines for the arms and legs with dots for the joints.

Hands

Hips

Add ovals for the hands.

Draw simple shapes for the hands and feet.

Feet

Use the construction lines to place the eyes, nose, mouth and ears.

Sketch in the shapes of the fingers and thumbs.

All the weight is supported on the right leg.

Changing the direction of the light source in a drawing can create drama and mood.

Add two lines for the wand.

Draw in the arms and legs using tube shapes. Use the dots to position the knees, ankles and elbows.

56

Add the wings.

Draw in the spiky hair and the pointed hairline.

Draw the neck and shoulders.

Sketch in the neck and sleeves of the tunic, curving them around the body.

Finish drawing the hands and fingers.

Add shading to the hair and wing patterns.

Sketch in the curved waistline and the hemline of the skirt.

Draw a star for the wand.

Sketch in the large, chunky boots.

Using the construction lines, draw a zigzag edging on the sleeves and neckline.

Give the skirt a zigzag hemline and draw lines up to the waist. Shade alternate panels where the light wouldn't reach.

Draw in the stripes around the arms and legs, and shade alternate stripes.

Remove any unwanted construction lines with an eraser.

Draw in the boot detail and shade them in.

57

DRAW Musical Fairies

Most fairies love to play music, the fairy flute being their favourite instrument. Throughout history, fairies have used music as a means of enchanting both animals and humans.

Draw two curved lines and a row of ovals for the shape of the flower wreath.

Add hair and place the neck and facial features.

Sketch in the hands around the flute.

Draw in the arms and legs using simple tube shapes.

Flower wreath

Add a line for the flute.

Draw in the flute.

Flute

Mark the centre of the head with two lines.

Draw in ovals for the head, body, hips and hands.

Draw in lines for the spine, shoulders and hips.

Add lines for the arms and legs with dots for the joints.

Draw triangular shapes for the feet.

Draw in the position of the big toe.

Draw two wings, making sure they are the same shape on either side.

Add petals to the wreath.

Add more detail to the face and hair.

Draw the flute shape.

Draw in the hands and fingers.

Add leaves and more detail to the flower wreath.

Finish the face and hair.

Start sketching in clothes, using simple shapes.

Sketch in the ankles and toes.

To finish the wings, draw in shapes like the veins of a butterfly's wings.

Shade the backs of both hands.

Add fold lines in the dress material.

Add shading to areas like this where light wouldn't reach.

Finish drawing the feet. Add toenails and ankles.

Remove any unwanted construction lines with an eraser.

59

DRAW
Fairy Friends

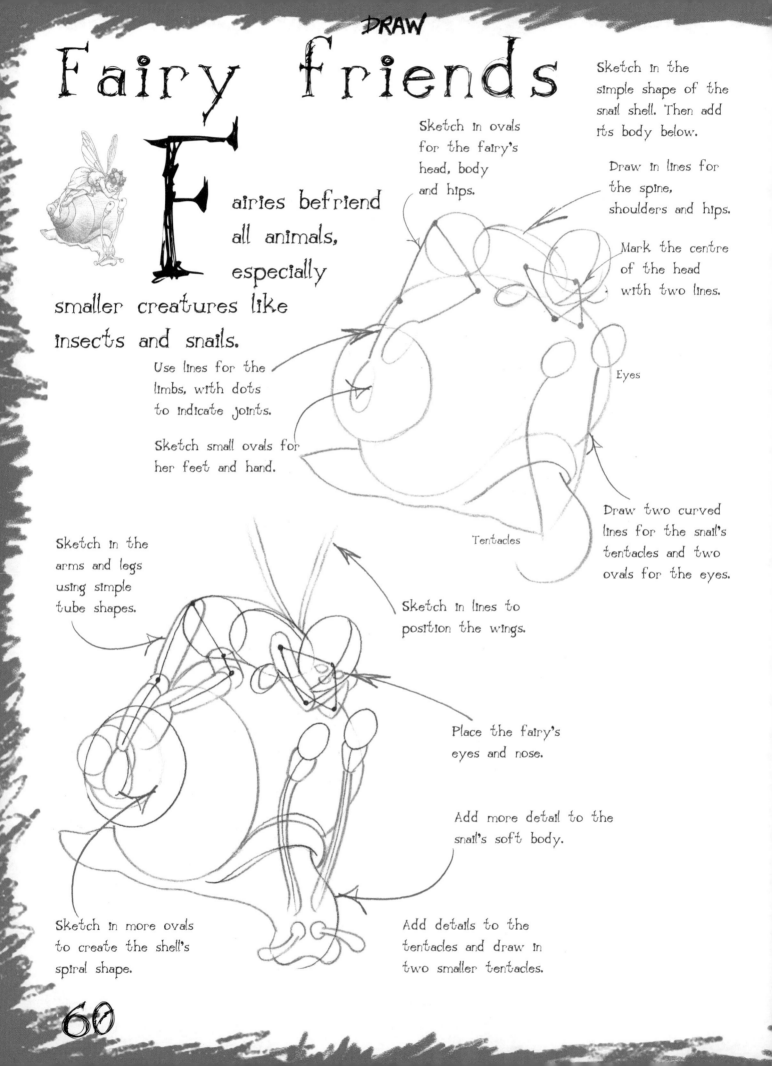

Fairies befriend all animals, especially smaller creatures like insects and snails.

Sketch in ovals for the fairy's head, body and hips.

Use lines for the limbs, with dots to indicate joints.

Sketch small ovals for her feet and hand.

Sketch in the simple shape of the snail shell. Then add its body below.

Draw in lines for the spine, shoulders and hips.

Mark the centre of the head with two lines.

Eyes

Tentacles

Draw two curved lines for the snail's tentacles and two ovals for the eyes.

Sketch in the arms and legs using simple tube shapes.

Sketch in lines to position the wings.

Place the fairy's eyes and nose.

Add more detail to the snail's soft body.

Sketch in more ovals to create the shell's spiral shape.

Add details to the tentacles and draw in two smaller tentacles.

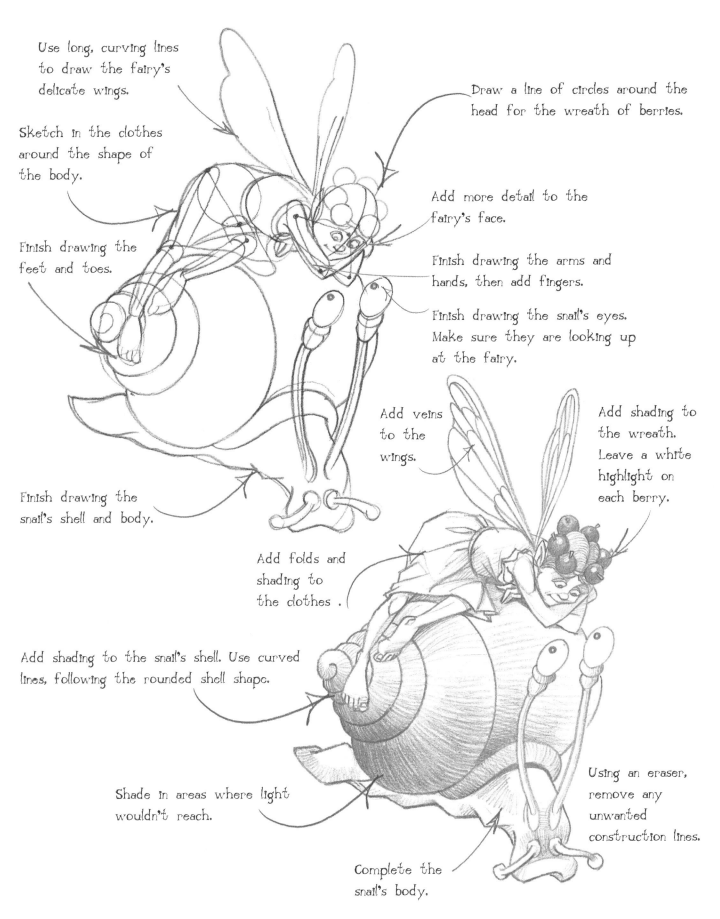

Use long, curving lines to draw the fairy's delicate wings.

Sketch in the clothes around the shape of the body.

Finish drawing the feet and toes.

Finish drawing the snail's shell and body.

Draw a line of circles around the head for the wreath of berries.

Add more detail to the fairy's face.

Finish drawing the arms and hands, then add fingers.

Finish drawing the snail's eyes. Make sure they are looking up at the fairy.

Add veins to the wings.

Add shading to the wreath. Leave a white highlight on each berry.

Add folds and shading to the clothes .

Add shading to the snail's shell. Use curved lines, following the rounded shell shape.

Shade in areas where light wouldn't reach.

Using an eraser, remove any unwanted construction lines.

Complete the snail's body.

61

DRAW Flying Fairies

Surprisingly, not all fairies are born with wings. Some fairies have their wings made from silken, spun gossamer, decorated with soft, downy feathers.

Look carefully at the angle and shape of the flying fairy before you start sketching her in.

Draw ovals for the head, body and hips.

Mark the centre of the head with two lines.

Draw in lines for the spine, shoulders and hips. Use these as a guide to position the arms and legs, adding dots for the joints.

Draw ovals for the hands and feet.

Use long curved lines to show the direction of the wings.

Wings

Place the facial features.

Draw in the arms and legs using simple tube shapes.

Draw in the shape of the hands and fingers.

Join the body to the hips with two curved lines.

Using more curved lines, draw the wings.

Sketch in the fairy's hat made of leaves and her spiky hair.

Add the shape of the ankle and draw in pointed pixie boots.

Add detail and shape to the face.

Sketch in leaves as clothing.

Add a bracelet.

Complete the wings, adding veins, a pattern and shading.

Add a zigzag edge to the leaf skirt and draw veins on it.

Add a belt.

Finish the face. Add shading to the eyes and a shadow under the hat to make her eyes stand out.

Finish the legs and boots.

Add shading to the hands.

Remove any unwanted construction lines using an eraser.

DRAW Fairy godmother

Rarely seen, fairy godmothers have very special, magical powers. Most children have a fairy godmother who has the power to help them, but alas, only once!

Mark the centre of the head with two lines.

Sketch in the hands and feet using simple shapes.

Draw in lines for the spine, shoulder and hips.

Head

Body

Hips

Draw in ovals for the head, body and shoulders.

Add lines for the arms and legs, with dots for the joints.

Place the facial features and the neck.

Add more detail to the hands, adding thumbs and fingers.

Draw in the arms and legs using simple tube shapes.

Sketch in the big toe.

Sketch in sharp, spiky wings.

Crown

Use long curved lines for the hair, then add a crown.

Add more detail to the facial features and draw in the shape of the face.

Add a bracelet.

Sketch in the clothes, giving shape to the bodice and waist.

Add shading to the hair and above the eyes. Use darker shading where the light wouldn't reach.

Finish off the fingers and hand shapes.

Add fold lines to the base of the skirt to show excess material.

Add veins and a pattern to the wings. Add shading to the edge of the wings.

Add detail to the bracelet and crown and draw in beads around her dress.

Add shading to areas of the bodice and skirt where light wouldn't reach.

Remove any unwanted construction lines using an eraser.

65

Woodland DRAW Fairies

Although the most numerous, woodland fairies are difficult to spot. Their ability to vanish into the undergrowth is legendary.

Look carefully at the angles and shape of this kneeling fairy.

Mark the centre of the head with two lines.

Head

Body

Hips

Feet

Draw in lines for the spine, shoulders and hips. Use these as a guide to position the ovals for the head, body and hips.

Add lines for the arms and legs with dots for joints (the head is positioned directly above the arms).

Hands

Carefully sketch in the shape and direction of the feet and hands.

Add the facial features.

Draw in the arms and legs using simple tube shapes.

Join the body to the hips.

Add thumbs to the hands.

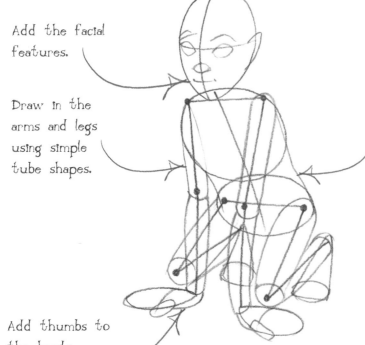

66

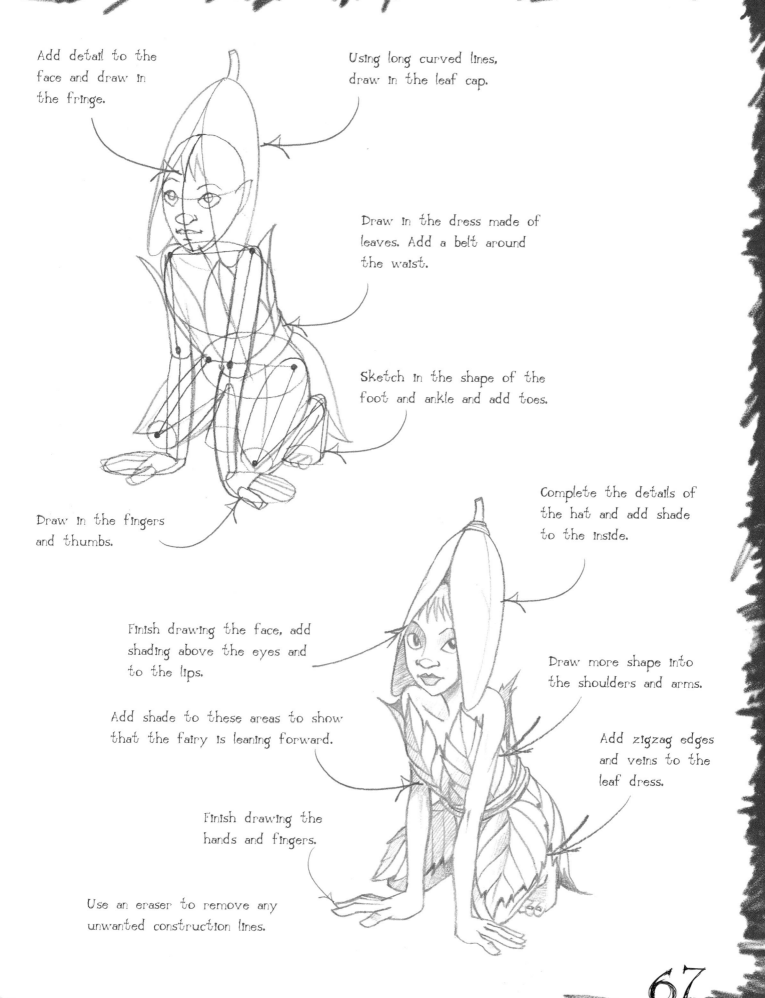

Add detail to the face and draw in the fringe.

Using long curved lines, draw in the leaf cap.

Draw in the dress made of leaves. Add a belt around the waist.

Sketch in the shape of the foot and ankle and add toes.

Draw in the fingers and thumbs.

Complete the details of the hat and add shade to the inside.

Finish drawing the face, add shading above the eyes and to the lips.

Draw more shape into the shoulders and arms.

Add shade to these areas to show that the fairy is leaning forward.

Add zigzag edges and veins to the leaf dress.

Finish drawing the hands and fingers.

Use an eraser to remove any unwanted construction lines.

67

Vampire

Vampires scour the night in search of unsuspecting victims to plunge their teeth into and suck their blood dry.

Draw in a circle for the head and two ovals for the torso and hips.

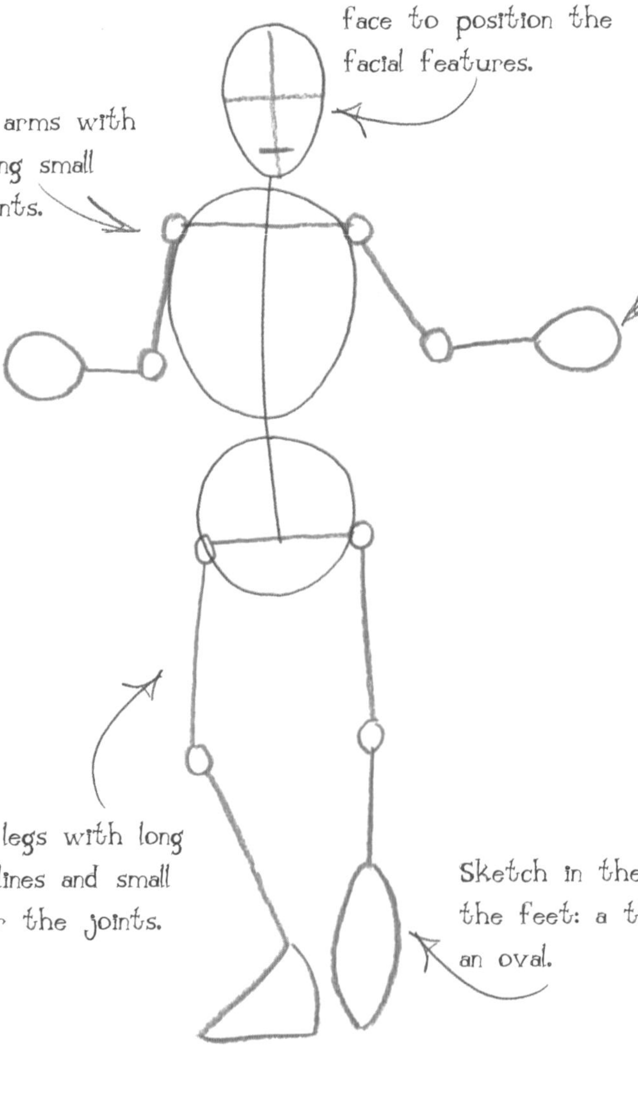

Head

Torso

Hips

Add construction lines to the face to position the facial features.

Draw the figure's arms with straight lines, adding small circles for the joints.

Add ovals for the hands.

Add the legs with long straight lines and small circles for the joints.

Sketch in the shape of the feet: a triangle and an oval.

Draw a simple candle in the vampire's hand.

Sketch in the facial features using the construction lines as a guide. Add the V-shaped hairline.

Add fingers to the oval hand.

Sketch in the shirt, adding cuffs and collar.

Draw the cape and collar using flowing curved lines.

Add the waistcoat and trousers with simple lines.

Complete the details of the face. Add tone to the hair and the mouth.

Draw in the chain using circles.

Add details to the candle and hands.

Add shading to areas light wouldn't reach.

Add buttons and details to the waistcoat.

Draw long curved lines for folds in the cape.

Finish the detail on the shoes.

Use an eraser to remove any unwanted construction lines.

DRAW

Zombie

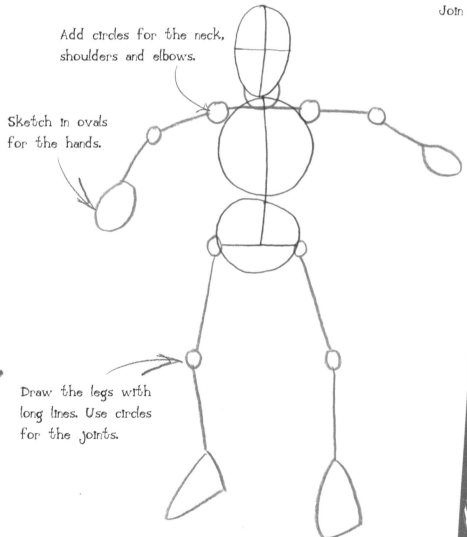

The 'dead' have risen and are walking the earth! The zombies will not stop until they have killed you and made you one of their own.

Sketch in basic construction lines to place facial features.

Head

Torso

Hips

Draw an oval for the head and two circles for the torso and hips. Join these with a centre line.

Add circles for the neck, shoulders and elbows.

Sketch in ovals for the hands.

Draw the legs with long lines. Use circles for the joints.

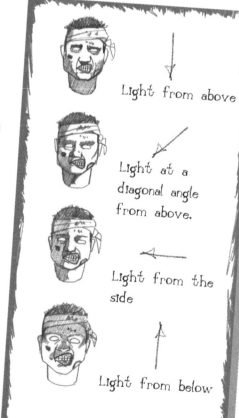

Light from above

Light at a diagonal angle from above.

Light from the side

Light from below

Changing the direction of the light source in a drawing can create drama and mood.

Start to sketch in the facial features.

Add the jacket and shirt around the figure using the construction lines as a guide.

Add a belt.

Add fingers to the hands.

Draw the trousers around the legs.

Finish the face, making it as scary as possible.

Add detail to the shoes.

Draw holes in the flesh with bone showing through.

Draw in the details of the jacket, adding rips and dirt marks.

Add shade to areas light doesn't reach.

Complete the details of the trousers.

Remove any unwanted construction lines with an eraser.

DRAW

Ghoul

Ghouls haunt graveyards or any other place where dead human flesh can be found. They devour the rotting meat, leaving nothing but the bones.

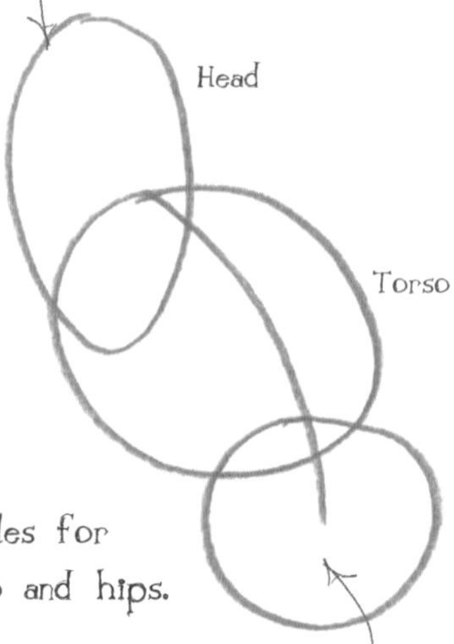

Draw a long oval for the head.

Head

Torso

Draw circles for the torso and hips.

Draw a curved line for the bent spine.

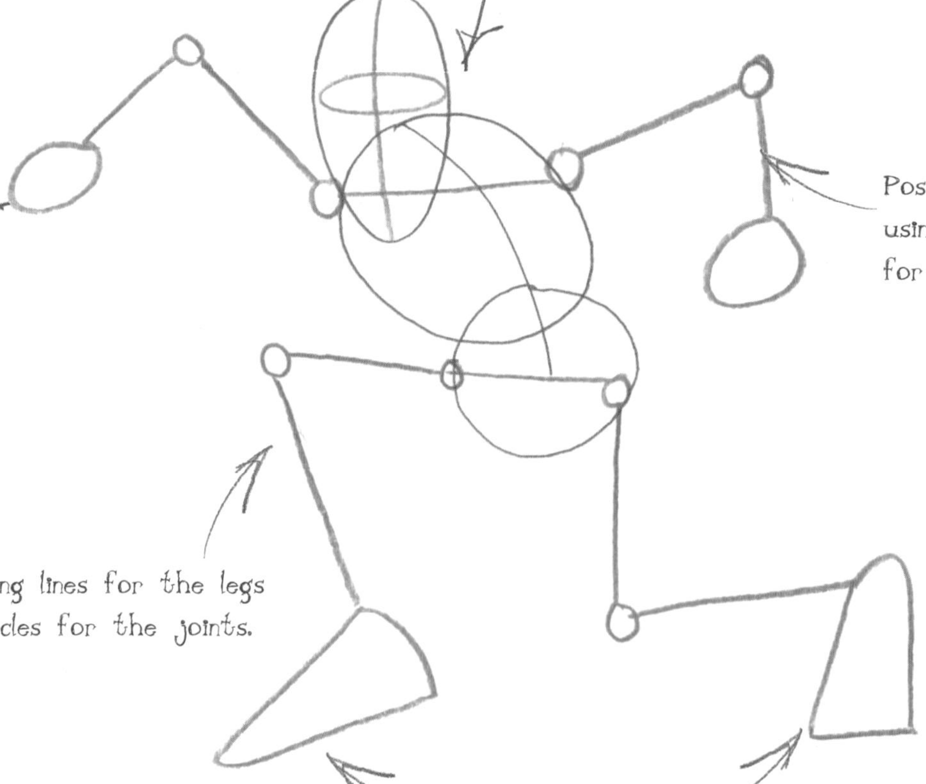

Add construction lines to the head to place the facial features.

Position the arms using lines and circles for the joints.

Sketch in ovals for the hands.

Add long lines for the legs and circles for the joints.

Draw in the creature's large feet.

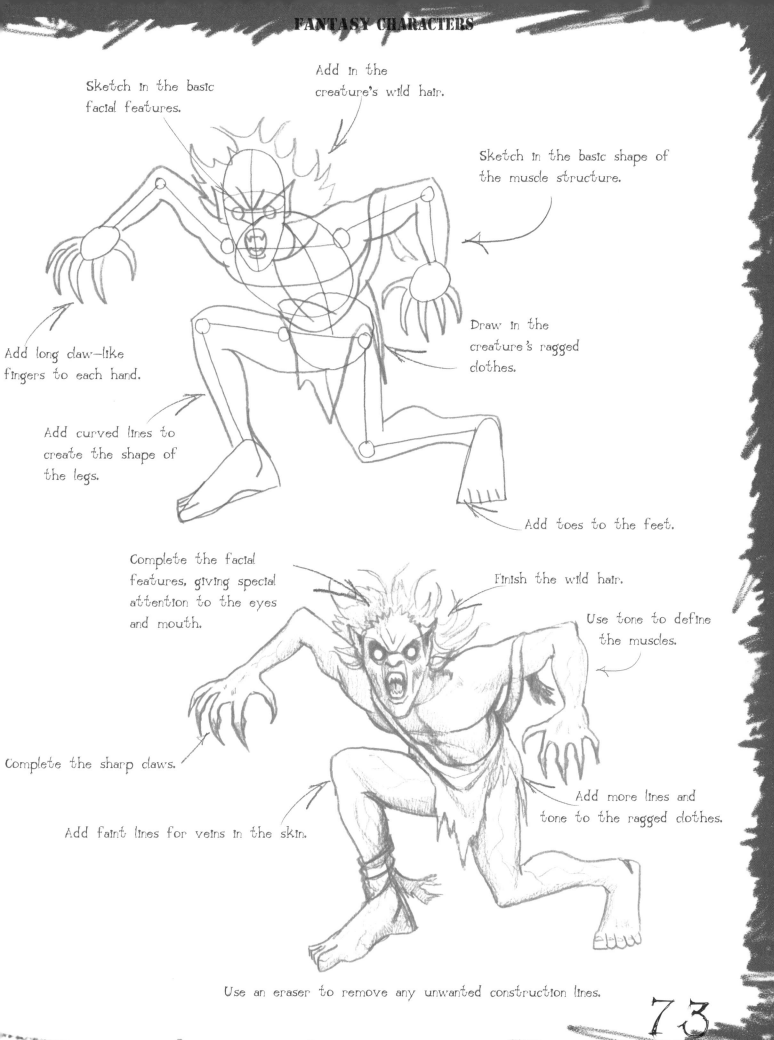

Sketch in the basic facial features.

Add in the creature's wild hair.

Sketch in the basic shape of the muscle structure.

Add long claw-like fingers to each hand.

Draw in the creature's ragged clothes.

Add curved lines to create the shape of the legs.

Add toes to the feet.

Complete the facial features, giving special attention to the eyes and mouth.

Finish the wild hair.

Use tone to define the muscles.

Complete the sharp claws.

Add more lines and tone to the ragged clothes.

Add faint lines for veins in the skin.

Use an eraser to remove any unwanted construction lines.

73

Werewolf DRAW If

Beware the full moon! Once this lunar phase is entered, these unassuming cursed people transform into creatures that are halfman and halfwolf, and will tear their victims apart!

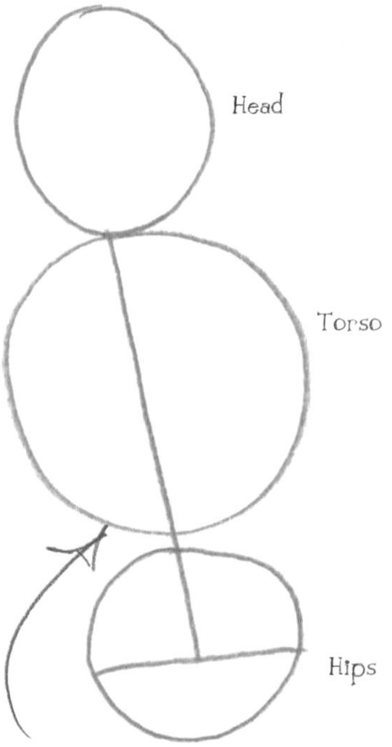

Head

Torso

Hips

Sketch an oval for the head and two circles for the torso and hips. Add a centre line for the spine and a line for the hips.

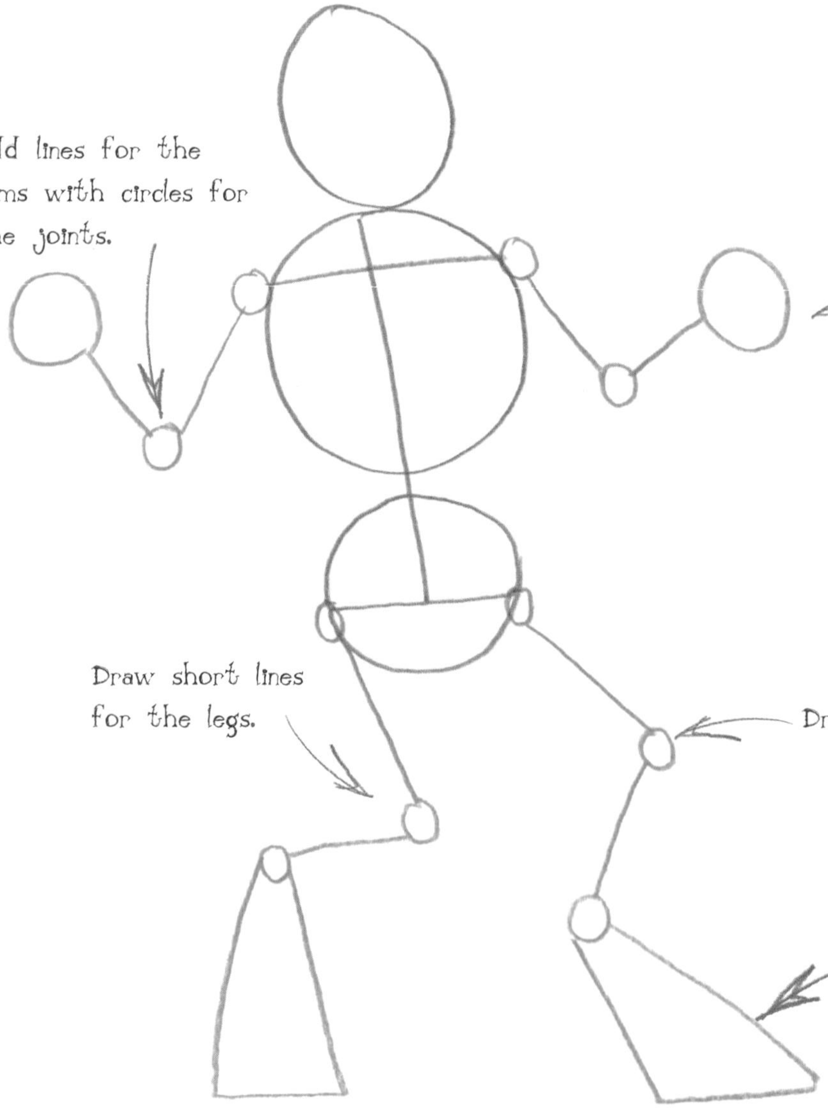

Add lines for the arms with circles for the joints.

Add circles for the hands.

Draw short lines for the legs.

Draw circles to indicate joints.

Add two large flipper-like feet.

Position the ear and eye.

Sketch in construction lines for the shape of the snout.

Add claws to the hands.

Join the head to the shoulders.

Finish the snout details and add sharp teeth.

Sketch in the ripped trousers.

Draw in the limbs using the construction lines as a guide.

Draw lots of short lines to indicate the fur.

Join the torso to the hips

Add the shape of the tail.

Complete the hands, adding pads and claws.

Add claws to the feet.

Finish the furry tail.

Complete the torn and ragged trousers.

Remove any unwanted construction lines with an eraser.

Draw in the details of the elongated feet.

75

Ghost

Ghosts are the souls of the dead who cannot rest. They haunt people at night, filling them with terror.

Sketch a construction line to place the eyes.

Add lines for the arms with circles for the joints.

Add ovals for the hands.

Head

Torso

Hips

Sketch three ovals for the head, torso and hips. Join these with a centre line for the spine.

Add long lines for the legs with circles for the joints.

Sketch in basic shapes for the feet.

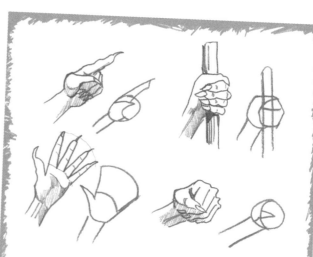

Practise sketching your own hands in different positions. This will help you draw characters with expressive hands.

Add pointed fingers.

Sketch in the arms using the construction lines as a guide.

Sketch in curved lines for the shape of the chest.

Add the outline of the body with long curved lines.

Add long, wavy lines for the hair.

Draw dark holes for the eyes, nostrils and mouth.

Draw in the legs using the construction lines as a guide.

Shade areas where light would not reach.

Draw lines to show the dress fabric hanging loosely on the figure.

Add straggly lines to create the ragged sleeves and hemline.

Remove any unwanted construction lines.

Draw in the toes.

Witch

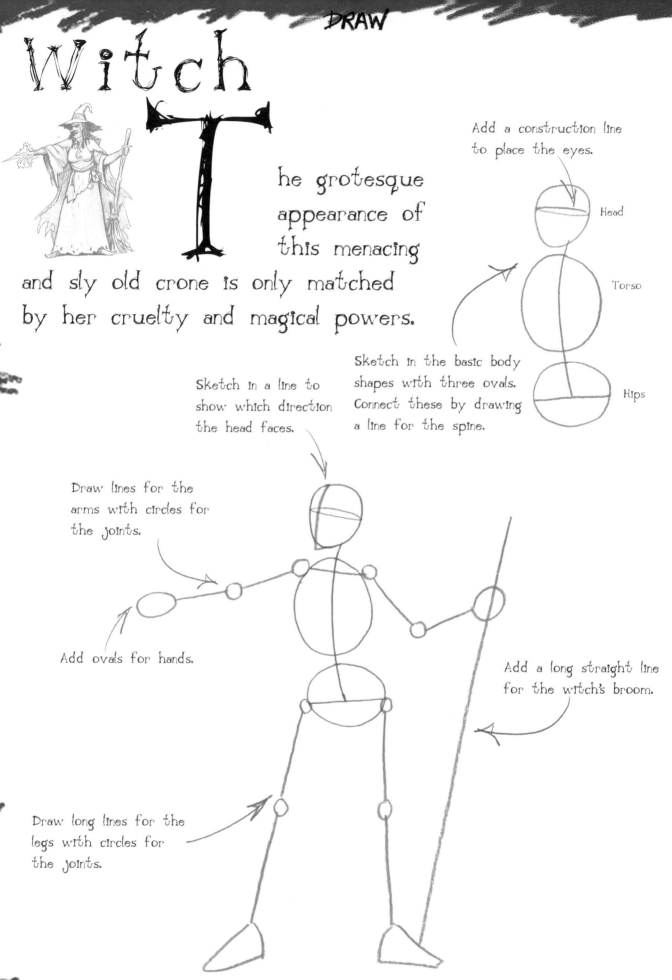

The grotesque appearance of this menacing and sly old crone is only matched by her cruelty and magical powers.

Add a construction line to place the eyes.

Head

Torso

Hips

Sketch in the basic body shapes with three ovals. Connect these by drawing a line for the spine.

Sketch in a line to show which direction the head faces.

Draw lines for the arms with circles for the joints.

Add ovals for hands.

Add a long straight line for the witch's broom.

Draw long lines for the legs with circles for the joints.

Add triangle shapes for the feet.

Draw in the shape of the witch's crooked hat.

Add basic facial features including a long nose!

Draw in the arms using the construction lines as a guide.

Draw this hand grasping the broom.

Draw long flaring lines for the clothes.

Add the shape of the broom bristles.

Complete the details and shading of the crooked hat.

Finish the ugly facial features.

Add ragged edges to her sleeves and clothes.

Draw sharp lines for magic shooting out of the witch's hand.

Add shading to areas where light won't reach.

Add trinkets to the witch's belt.

Add tears and holes to the clothing.

Using an eraser, remove any unwanted construction lines.

DRAW
Frankenstein's creature

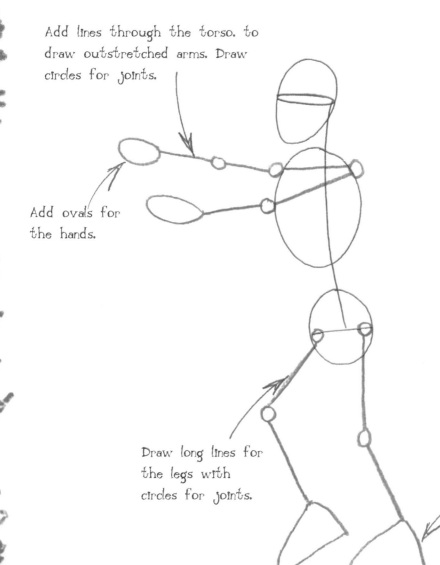

Victor Frankenstein plundered body parts to create an undead being in a terrifying electrical experiment. This man-made creature walks the night alone.

Head

Torso

Hips

Draw in the position of the eyes.

Draw two ovals for the head and torso and a circle for the hips. Draw in a centre line and a horizontal line for the hips.

Add lines through the torso. to draw outstretched arms. Draw circles for joints.

Add ovals for the hands.

Draw long lines for the legs with circles for joints.

Sketch in two triangles for the feet.

Draw lots of small stick figures to find the best action pose. Try posing in front of a mirror to work out what looks best.

Draw fingers on the hands.

Add basic facial features.

Sketch in the hair.

Add a bolt through the neck.

Sketch in the basic shape of the jacket. Make the sleeves look short.

Add a pocket to the jacket.

Draw the trousers and belt using the construction lines as a guide.

Finish the details of the head.

Add some details to the shoes.

Add shading to areas that light won't reach.

Draw patches on the knee and elbow.

Draw the laces and extra detail on the shoes.

Use an eraser to remove any unwanted construction lines.

81

Scarecrow

This frightening character bursts into life at Halloween, scaring innocent bystanders and terrorising nearby towns.

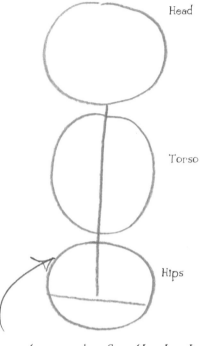

Head

Torso

Hips

Draw two circles for the head and hips and an oval for the torso. Add a curved line for the spine and a horizontal line at the hips.

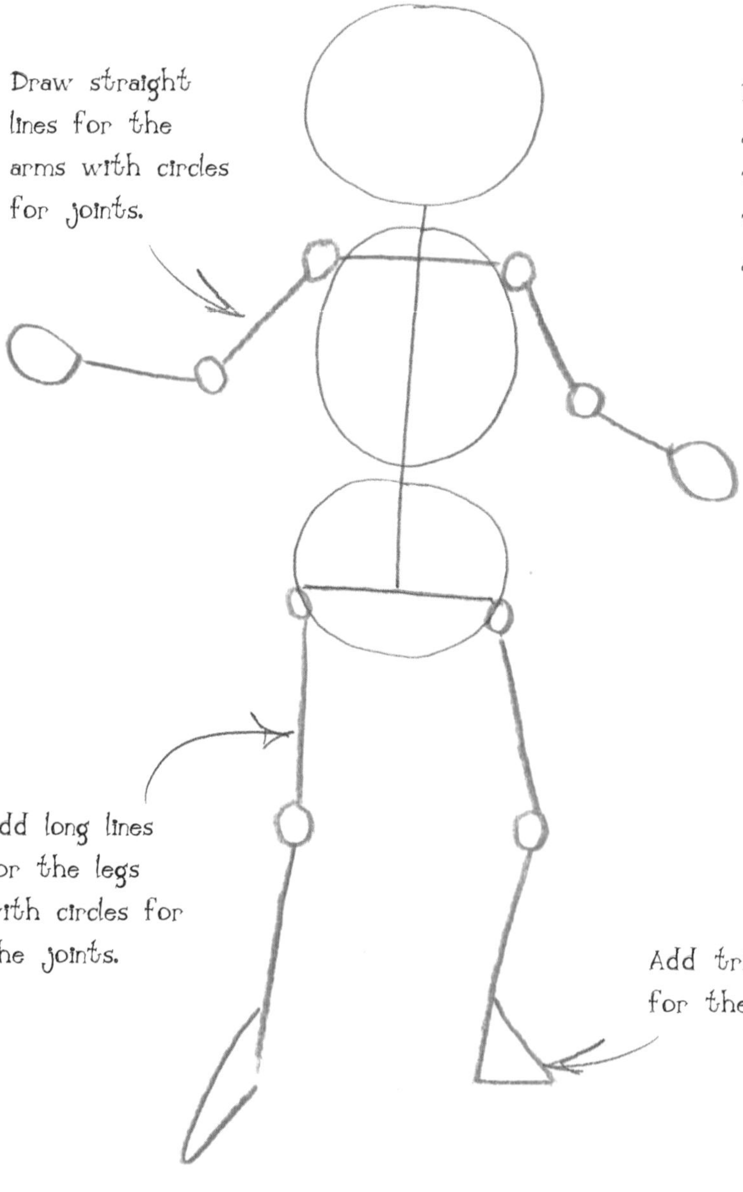

Draw straight lines for the arms with circles for joints.

Add ovals for the hands.

Add long lines for the legs with circles for the joints.

Add triangle shapes for the feet.

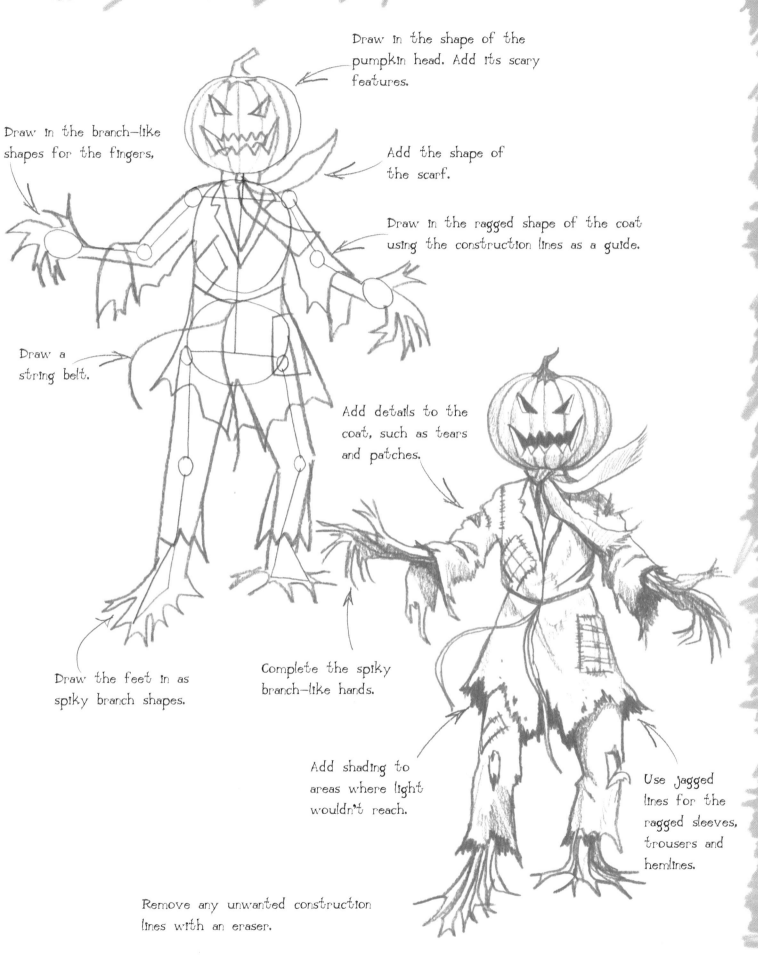

Draw in the shape of the pumpkin head. Add its scary features.

Draw in the branch-like shapes for the fingers,

Add the shape of the scarf.

Draw in the ragged shape of the coat using the construction lines as a guide.

Draw a string belt.

Add details to the coat, such as tears and patches.

Draw the feet in as spiky branch shapes.

Complete the spiky branch-like hands.

Add shading to areas where light wouldn't reach.

Use jagged lines for the ragged sleeves, trousers and hemlines.

Remove any unwanted construction lines with an eraser.

DRAW
The Grim Reaper

Hope you don't meet up with this cloaked figure any time soon! His appearance means your life has come to an end, as he has come to collect your soul.

Head

Torso

Hips

Draw in rounded shapes for the head, neck, torso and hips. Add a line for the spine.

Sketch in the construction lines for the facial features.

Draw a long curved line for the scythe.

Draw straight lines for the arms with circles for the joints.

Add ovals for the hands.

Sketch in long lines for the legs with circles for the joints.

Sketch in the shapes of the feet.

Draw the basic skull features.

Draw the shape of the head inside a loose-fitting hood.

Add curved lines for the blade.

Add the long, open sleeves of the cloak.

Sketch in bony fingers holding the scythe.

Add jagged lines for the flowing edges of the cape and the hemline.

Finish the skull details.

Add lines to create the bony feet.

Complete the details of the scythe.

Add shading to areas where light would not reach.

Draw in a pile of skulls and bones.

Add tonal lines for folds in the cloak.

Use an eraser to remove any unwanted construction lines.

85

DRAW
Blackbeard

A fearsome pirate who terrorised all who sailed the Caribbean Seas. He carried six loaded pistols and famously tucked smouldering lit fuses under his hat so that the smoke would make him look even scarier.

Draw ovals for the head, body and hips.

Head

Add straight lines for the shoulders and hips.

Body

Hips

Add ears and facial details.

Add the arms and legs with dots to show the joints.

Draw in ovals for the knees.

Sketch in simple shapes for the hands and feet.

Draw in the shape of the musket.

Add shape to the feet.

Draw in the shape of the hat and clothing.

Sketch in the beard, moustache and hair.

Sketch in the sword and pistols.

Finish the beard and add shading.

Add details to the musket.

Add the shape of the shoes.

Shade all areas where light wouldn't reach.

Finish off all the details of the clothing. Add ragged edges and tears.

Add detail to his weapons.

Add buckles to his shoes and complete all details.

Remember to remove any unwanted construction lines.

Pirate with DRAW parrot

The exotic animals that pirates found as they travelled around the world made excellent companions on board ship. Parrots could even be taught to speak!

Draw an oval for the head.

Draw a vertical ellipse through the centre of the oval.

Draw a horizontal ellipse through the centre of the oval to position the eyes.

Add the nose, mouth and ears.

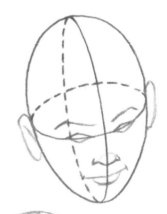

Draw in ovals for the parrot's head and body.

Sketch in the shoulders using curved lines.

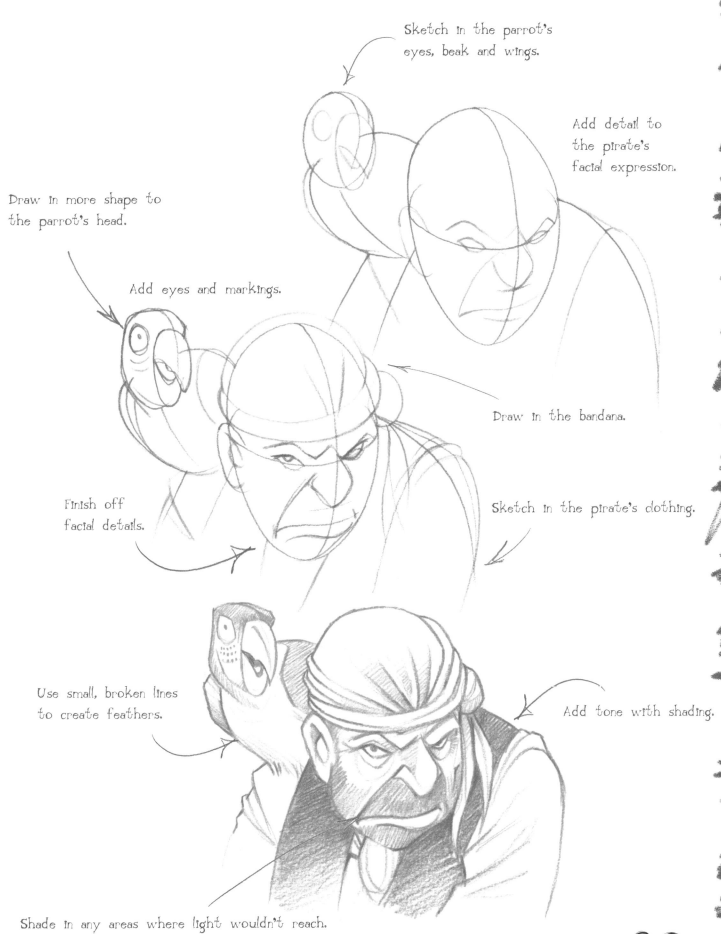

Sketch in the parrot's eyes, beak and wings.

Add detail to the pirate's facial expression.

Draw in more shape to the parrot's head.

Add eyes and markings.

Draw in the bandana.

Finish off facial details.

Sketch in the pirate's clothing.

Use small, broken lines to create feathers.

Add tone with shading.

Shade in any areas where light wouldn't reach.

89

Buccaneer

Armed to the teeth, this cut-throat pirate is ready to attack. This pose captures a sense of action and excitement.

Sketch in ovals for the head, body and hips. Add straight lines for the shoulders and hips.

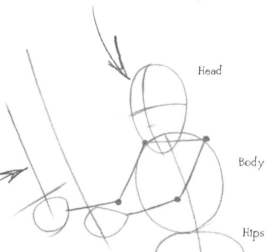

Head

Body

Hips

Add shapes for hands and feet.

Draw in straight lines for the arms and legs.

Add lines for a cutlass in one hand and a dagger in the other.

Draw the hat in around the head.

Use curved lines to add shape to the blades. Draw in handles.

Add the ears and position the facial features.

Using the construction lines as a guide, start drawing in the main shapes of the body.

Sketch in tube shapes for the arms and legs with dots for joints.

Add more shape to the feet.

Add detail to the structure of the hat.

Draw in hair using flowing lines.

Draw in the eyes, nose, ears and mouth.

Add the fingers and thumbs.

Use curved, sweeping lines to draw in the swirl of the topcoat to show movement.

Draw in cuffs on sleeves.

Add large cuffs to the top of the boots.

Add shading to the hat and belt.

Complete the details of the cutlass and dagger.

Add pockets, buttonholes, buttons and patterned cuffs.

Shade all the areas where light wouldn't reach.

Add buckles to the boots.

91

Pirates in action

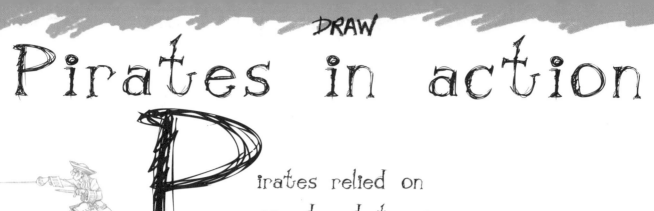

Pirates relied on speed and terror to attack their victim's ship. Once on board they fought with great fury. This action pose captures the cut and thrust of the attack.

Draw ovals for the head, body and hips of both figures.

Sketch in the straight lines for the arms and legs with dots for joints.

Sketch straight lines for the weapons.

Add simple shapes for the hands and feet.

Note the angle of the feet.

Position the eyes, nose and ears.

Using the construction lines as a guide, draw in the main shapes of the bodies.

Draw in the tube shapes for the arms and legs.

Add fingers and thumbs to the hands.

Add details to the weapons.

Draw in the hat shapes curving around the head.

Sketch large cuffs on the coat.

Add tall over-the-knee boots.

Draw in boots with a fold over the top.

Add detail to the faces and hair.

Draw in all the finishing details to the clothing and boots.

Finish off the daggers and swords.

Add shading to the areas that light wouldn't reach.

Add detail to the faces and hair.

Add buckles.

Remove any unwanted construction lines.

Glossary

Chiaroscuro The practice of drawing high-contrast pictures with a lot of black and white, but not much grey.

Composition The arrangement of the parts of a picture on the drawing paper.

Construction lines Guidelines used in the early stages of a drawing. They are usually erased later.

Fixative A type of resin used to spray over a finished drawing to prevent smudging. **It should only be used by an adult.**

Focal point A central point of interest.

Foreshortening Drawing part of a figure shorter than it really is, so it looks as though it is pointing towards the viewer.

Light source The direction from which the light seems to come in a drawing.

Perspective A method of drawing in which near objects are shown larger than faraway objects to give an impression of depth.

Pose The position assumed by a figure.

Proportion The correct relationship of scale between each part of the drawing.

Silhouette A drawing that shows only a flat, dark shape, like a shadow.

Three-dimensional Having an effect of depth, so as to look lifelike or real.

Vanishing point The place in a perspective drawing where parallel lines appear to meet.

Index